Beijing Tour Guide:
Cartoons
Wang Qicheng

China Intercontinental Press

About Qii

Chinese name: Qí Qí

English name: Qii

Character: open, confident

Hobbies: reading, music, traveling, chatting

Favorite sports: football, basketball, tennis, table tennis

Pet phrase: What a beauty!

Favorite food: Chinese cuisine

Favorite dress: traditional Chinese clothes

Favorite colors: red, orange, yellow, green, white, blue, purple

Best buddy: Lín Lín (Liin)

Favorite place: seashore

Qii is curious of everything like a child. He loves Chinese culture and has many dreams. He is fond of studying, of life and of friends. He is gifted with an easy-going attitude and takes everything positively, a nature that is longed for by urbanites under increasing burdens of busy modern life. Qii believes in "freedom of oneself". He nurtures a beautiful dream: One day, he could be the "cartoon ambassador" to promote the profound traditional Chinese culture, modern life and the aspiring attitude of today's Chinese people in a leisurely and joyful way.

Fascinating city

Beijing drew the whole world's attention with the 2008 Olympics. But it is also an ancient city that has been the nation's capital for 850 years in its total history of more than 3,000 years. It is a great city with the magnitude of a vast country and the hustle and bustle of a thriving cosmopolis. It is home to the humorous Beijingers, who take immense pride in world-known landmarks like the Forbidden City and the Great Wall. The long, glorious history has brought Beijing an air that is elegant, unconventional, yet reserved; the fast-developing economy and culture have never stopped making facelifts to the old city. The interesting and amazing contrast between the old and new has enticed numerous people to admire and experience the city's unique charm.

Contents

Capital of culture

P.042

Bustling city life

P. 104

Beijing for gourmets

P. 122

Beijing folk culture

P. 136

Beijing's
past

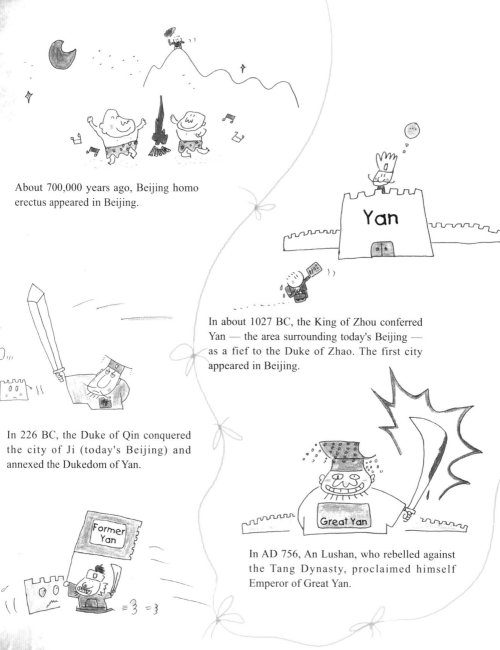

About 700,000 years ago, Beijing homo erectus appeared in Beijing.

In about 1027 BC, the King of Zhou conferred Yan — the area surrounding today's Beijing — as a fief to the Duke of Zhao. The first city appeared in Beijing.

In 226 BC, the Duke of Qin conquered the city of Ji (today's Beijing) and annexed the Dukedom of Yan.

In AD 756, An Lushan, who rebelled against the Tang Dynasty, proclaimed himself Emperor of Great Yan.

In AD 350, the Former Yan Dynasty conquered the city of Ji and made it its capital.

In AD 911, Liu Shouguang proclaimed himself Emperor of the Great North and took Ji as the capital.

In AD 938, Liao Dynasty renamed Youzhou Prefecture (today's Beijing) as its Southern Capital (also a secondary capital).

In 1153, Emperor Hailin of Jin Dynasty moved the capital to Yanjing (today's Beijing) and changed the name to Zhongdu (Middle Capital).

In 1215, Mongolian troops captured the Middle Capital.

In 1272, Yuan Dynasty changed the Middle Capital to Dadu (Grand Capital), and made it the national capital.

In 1368, Ming Dynasty troops conquered Dadu and renamed it Beiping Prefecture.

In 1403, Emperor Yongle of Ming Dynasty named Beiping as "Beijing" (Northern Capital, also known as Peking).

In 1406, Emperor Yongle issued the decree to move the capital to Beijing.

In 1407, constructions of palaces, temples and other architectures began.

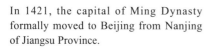

In 1421, the capital of Ming Dynasty formally moved to Beijing from Nanjing of Jiangsu Province.

In 1564, the outer city of Beijing was completed.

In 1644, Qing Dynasty moved its capital to Beijing.

In 1860, the British and French troops invaded Beijing and burned down Yuanmingyuan, the imperial garden near the Summer Palace.

In 1900, the Eight-Nation Alliance invaded Beijing.

In 1912, Emperor Xuantong of Qing Dynasty abdicated, marking the end of the Qing Dynasty.

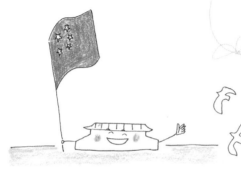

In 1949, the People's Republic of China was founded with Beijing as its capital.

impression
of Beijingers

Characters of Beijingers

Warm, sanguine, humorous, sincere, magnanimous, experienced and knowledgeable, Beijingers are gifted with a touch of kindness, fond of chatting and love to defend their "faces". Beijing ladies are elegant and tasteful.

Say it if you need me.

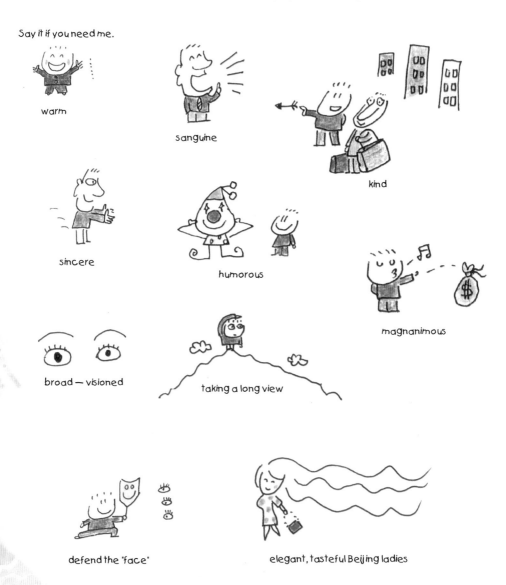

warm

sanguine

kind

sincere

humorous

magnanimous

broad — visioned

taking a long view

defend the "face"

elegant, tasteful Beijing ladies

Beijingers are good at banter

"kan"(侃):banter

Banter is an important part of Beijingers' humor. With good-natured raillery, Beijingers are fond of exchanging light, playful and teasing remarks that are full of passion for life.

A taste of Beijing dialect

Beijing dialect — *jing qiang* — is musical, expressive and easy to understand. The standard Chinese, or *putonghua*, and pinyin are based on the Beijing dialect. The most impressive feature of Beijing dialect is the suffix "*er*". Here are some examples:

Jīnr : today

Dou jī língr: be boastful, a derogatory term

Māor ni: a dark secret kept from everyone

Dòu le: joking

Shuàn rén: play tricks on others, fail to keep one's word

Could you send a letter for me, please?

Láo jià: ask someone for favor

Cuō huǒr: be angry but do not let it out

Strong, reliable relationship

Cí shi: solid, strong, reliable

Tào cí: network, trying to establish a relationship for one's own benefit

Bié jie: don't do that

Méi zhé: nothing can be done
Huáng le: to no avail

Pín zuǐ: speak garrulously

We are very close together.

Bèir hao: very good

Liu wānr: take a walk

Tǒng lóu zi: invite trouble

I must go.

Diǎnr: take leave

Kǎn yé: someone who is boastful

Bāi le: the relationship is broken

Kōu ménr: stingy, avaricious

Yóur:
wily, well versed in ways of the world

Liu zǎo:
morning exercises

Nà zhǔr: someone who shouldn't be offended

Dòu mèn zi: joking

Zán liǎ shuí gēn shuí:
We are on very close terms

sculpture   *Suí suí:* beauty

Mǎn shì jiè: everywhere

Dà lǎo yé menr: men

Bá fènr: excel

Liàn: confront

Gē menr: buddies

Sights of
a big nation

Tian'anmen Square

At the center of Beijing, the Tian'anmen Square is big enough for 1 million people to gather together. Measuring 880 m from north to south and 500 m from east to west, the 440,000 sq m square is the biggest of its kind in the world. The Tian'anmen Rostrum lies to the north of the majestic square, with the National Museum of China to its east and the Great Hall of the People to its west.

Flag-raising ceremony

The flag-raising ceremony held every morning upon sunrise at the northern rim of the Tian'anmen Square has become one of the nation's symbolic sights. It is held at the moment when the sun rises over the East Sea of China, which means that the country is growing stronger like the rising sun. The team of 96 PLA soldiers who guard the national flag symbolizes the upholding of the 9.6 million sq km of China's territory. Dressed in dashing uniform, the ceremonial guards follow a flag bearer and two flag-raisers. Accompanied by the military music, they walk across the Golden Water Bridge and march in exactly 138 steps before reaching the flag post. The flag-raising ceremony best represents the spirit of the Chinese nation.

Mao Zedong Memorial Hall

Lying to the south of the Monument to the People's Heroes on the Tian'anmen Square, the memorial is where Mao Zedong (1893-1976), the founder of New China, rests. It is a sacred site for the Chinese. Finished in May 1977, the cubic hall has 44 granite columns outside. In the middle of the staircases outside the northern and southern gates, sunflower, Japanese rohdea, wintersweet and pine are sculpted on the white marble boards.

Monument to the People's Heroes

Erected at the center of the Tian'anmen Square, the Monument to the People's Heroes commemorates the martyrs who sacrificed their lives for the nation in modern Chinese history. Standing at 37.94 m tall, the monument's base is composed of two parts. The upper part is square and formed with two layers of pedestals. The lower pedestal is inlaid with eight white marble relief sculptures that display famous events in the past century. In 1839, Qing Dynasty official Lin Zexu banned opium and burned all confiscated opium in Guangzhou, which led to the two Opium Wars (1840-1842), marking the beginning of Western powers' invasion of China; the Jintian Uprising in 1851 that grew into the Taiping Heavenly Kingdom; the Wuchang Uprising in 1911 that eventually toppled the Qing Dynasty and ended China's feudal history; the May Fourth Movement in 1919 that has become China's Youth Day; the May 30th Movement in 1925 led by the Chinese Communist Party against Japanese imperialists; the Nanchang Uprising on Aug 1, 1927 led by the Chinese Communist Party; the guerrilla war in the War of Resistance Against Japanese Aggression (1937-1945); and the crossing of the Yangtze River by the People's Liberation Army (PLA) in 1949. On both sides of the last scene, there are two smaller scenes with the themes of "sending materials to the soldiers on the frontline" and "welcoming the PLA". The relief sculptures are 2 m high and feature more than 170 figures.

Eternal glory to the people's heroes!

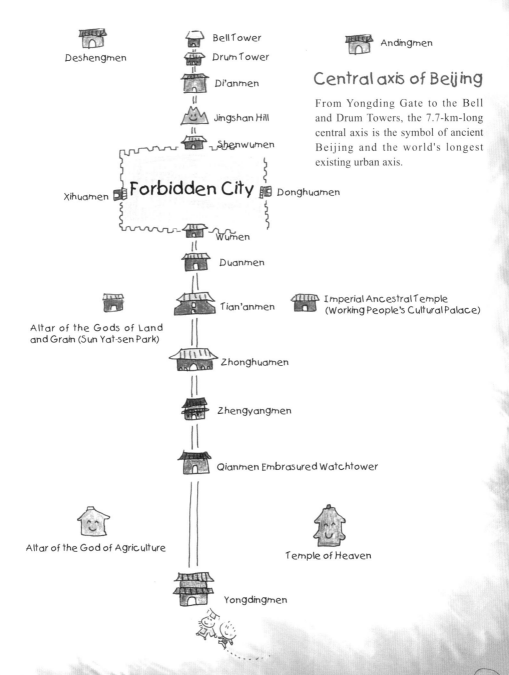

Deshengmen

Bell Tower

Drum Tower

Andingmen

Di'anmen

Central axis of Beijing

From Yongding Gate to the Bell and Drum Towers, the 7.7-km-long central axis is the symbol of ancient Beijing and the world's longest existing urban axis.

Jingshan Hill

Shenwumen

Xihuamen **Forbidden City** Donghuamen

Wumen

Duanmen

Altar of the Gods of Land and Grain (Sun Yat-sen Park)

Tian'anmen

Imperial Ancestral Temple (Working People's Cultural Palace)

Zhonghuamen

Zhengyangmen

Qianmen Embrasured Watchtower

Altar of the God of Agriculture

Temple of Heaven

Yongdingmen

Great Hall of the People

Lying to the west of the Tian'anmen Square, the Great Hall of the People is the venue for the country's most important meetings such as the National People's Congress. Besides the grand meeting hall with a capacity of 10,000 seats and a dinning hall of 5,000 seats, the venue is also famous for 34 halls named after all the provinces, municipalities, autonomous regions and the special administrative regions. It only took ten months to complete the grand architecture in 1959.

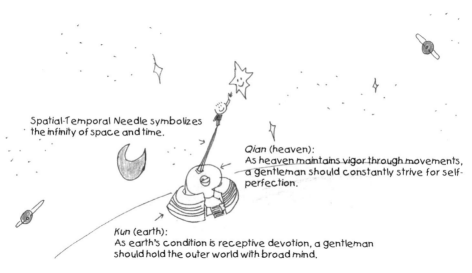

Spatial-Temporal Needle symbolizes the infinity of space and time.

Qian (heaven):
As heaven maintains vigor through movements, a gentleman should constantly strive for self-perfection.

Kun (earth):
As earth's condition is receptive devotion, a gentleman should hold the outer world with broad mind.

China Millennium Monument Museum

Built on the western Chang'an Avenue to commemorate the new millennium, the China Millennium Monument Museum is formed with the main building, bronze passage and holy fire plaza. With the theme of "harmony", it is a symbol of the harmonious development of man and nature, as well as the harmonious integration of Eastern and Western cultures. The design of the altar features water and stone in poetic and symbolic language. The deep-set plaza and bronze passage are decorated with flowing streams; the altar, plaza and passage are built with 40,000 sq m of cream-colored granite. The 270-m-long bronze passage is carved with the timeline between the appearance of humans and the year 2000. The main building consists of the Millennium Hall, Gallery of Eastern and Western Arts, Modern Arts Gallery and Multi-Media Digital Art Gallery. The perimeter of the circular mural inside the Millennium Hall is 117 m, making it the biggest of its kind in China.

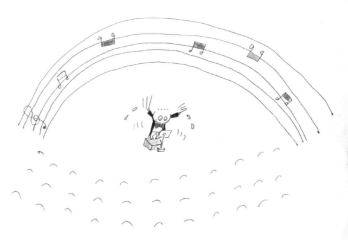

National Center for Performing Arts

To the west of the Great Hall of the People is the National Center for Performing Arts. Designed by French architect Paul Andreu, it is the world's biggest domed architecture. Many high-level performances are staged here.

National Museum of China

Lying to the east of Tian'anmen Square, the National Museum of China is the museum of the highest level in the country. Displayed according to chronology, the cultural relics capture the 5,000 years of Chinese civilization. Besides carrying out archaeological excavations, the museum collects, studies and displays cultural relics. The prided collection with the museum reflects the splendid ancient, modern and contemporary history of China. Wandering in the spacious halls of the museum is like sailing down a mighty river of the past 5,000 years that shaped China.

sights of
the imperial
capital

Tian'anmen Rostrum

Lying at the heart of Beijing, the Tian'anmen Rostrum was first built in 1417 of the Ming Dynasty as Chengtianmen. In 1651, it was renamed Tian'anmen, meaning "granted by the heavens to bring peace and order to the nation". Emperors used to issue decrees here in major ceremonies. The rostrum used

Imperial
Decree

to have five towers on either side to mark its supreme status. Its width equals that of nine standard rooms and its depth equals that of five rooms. The rostrum has multiple roofs shaped like a mountain. In front of it is the Golden Water River spanned by five white marble bridges with refined carvings. Sitting on both sides of the rostrum are two stone lions and the ornamental columns known as *huabiao*. The Tian'anmen Rostrum is the symbol of China. Today, its gates are kept open for visitors from far and wide.

Imperial Ancestral Temple (Working People's Cultural Palace)

Situated to the east of Tian'anmen Rostrum, the Imperial Ancestral Temple has become the Working People's Cultural Palace. In the Ming and Qing dynasties (1368-1911), the temple was the venue for grand ceremonies to pay tribute to ancestors when emperors ascended the throne, assumed the reins of government, married and returned to the capital after a victorious war. The temple's main buildings are the three great halls that face the Daji Gate. Outside

Ancestor

the gate is the Jade Belt River and Golden Water Bridge. On eastern and western sides to the north of the bridge are two hexagon pavilions that shelter wells. To the south of the bridge are the Sacred Kitchen and Sacred Warehouse. To their south is a colorful glazed door. Outside are the slaughter house and another pavilion covering a well.

Altar of the Gods of Land and Grain (Sun Yat-sen Park)

Lying to the west of Tian'anmen Rostrum, the altar was first built in 1421 in the Ming Dynasty as a place for the emperors to pay tribute to the Gods of Land and Grain and pray for bumper harvest. For centuries, emperors regarded land and grain (*sheji* in Chinese) as symbols of the nation. Feudal emperors called themselves sons of heaven. They picked an early morning in spring and autumn to pay tribute at the altar. Similar ceremonies were held when imperial troops were launched to the battlefield and returned to the capital, bringing captives. Disasters like floods also warranted sacrificial ceremonies at the altar. The altar is covered with earth of five colors: yellow in the center, blue in the east, red in the south, white in the west and black in the north — to symbolize that "every corner in the world belongs to the emperor".

Zhengyang Gate

First built in 1419 of the Ming Dynasty, the Zhengyang Gate was called Lizheng Gate. As it is located to the south of the Forbidden City, it is also called Qianmen (Front Gate). It is one of the nine most important gates in Beijing. The gate is actually formed with three parts — the gate, the embrasured watchtower over the gate and the citadel outside the gate to reinforce its defense. The grand complex is a representative of ancient Beijing architecture. It is the only intact city gate in Beijing. The gate has been turned into the Museum on Beijing's Folk Customs.

33

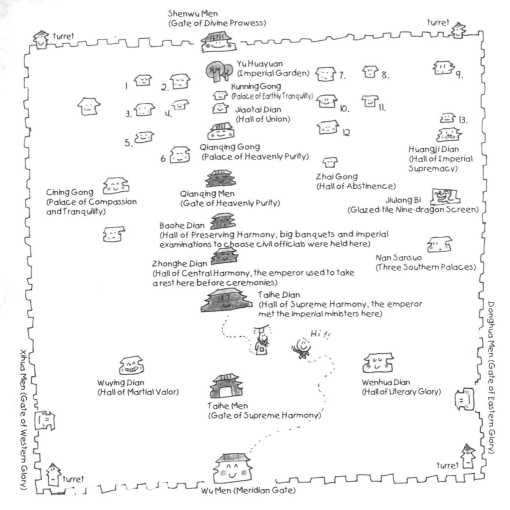

Shenwu Men
(Gate of Divine Prowess)

turret

turret

Yu Huayuan
(Imperial Garden)

1.   2.   7.   8.   9.

Kunning Gong
(Palace of Earthly Tranquility)

3.   4.   Jiaotai Dian
(Hall of Union)   10.   11.

5.   12

Qianqing Gong
6   (Palace of Heavenly Purity)   13.

Huangji Dian
(Hall of Imperial
Supremacy)

Cining Gong
(Palace of Compassion
and Tranquility)

Qianqing Men
(Gate of Heavenly Purity)

Zhai Gong
(Hall of Abstinence)

Jiulong Bi
(Glazed-tile Nine-dragon Screen)

Baohe Dian
(Hall of Preserving Harmony, big banquets and imperial
examinations to choose civil officials were held here)

Zhonghe Dian
(Hall of Central Harmony, the emperor used to take
a rest here before ceremonies)

Nan Sansuo
(Three Southern Palaces)

Taihe Dian
(Hall of Supreme Harmony, the emperor
met the imperial ministers here)

Hi !!

Wuying Dian
(Hall of Martial Valor)

Wenhua Dian
(Hall of Literary Glory)

Taihe Men
(Gate of Supreme Harmony)

Xihua Men (Gate of Western Glory)

Donghua Men (Gate of Eastern Glory)

turret

turret

Wu Men (Meridian Gate)

Palace Museum

At the center of Beijing, the Palace Museum is built on the basis of the imperial palace, or the Forbidden City, in the Ming and Qing dynasties. Reputed with 9,999 rooms, the palace is the world's biggest and most intact complex of ancient architecture. The front gate of the Forbidden City is the Tian'anmen Rostrum, and the Shenwu (Divine Prowess) Gate is its back door. Established in 1420 of the Ming Dynasty, a total of 24 emperors lived here and ruled China for nearly 500 years. The museum has a collection of 1 million artifacts, most of which are imperial relics such as the imperial thrones and classic art works.

Prince Gong's Residence

At the Liuyin Street to the west of Shichahai Park, Prince Gong's Residence is the biggest of the remaining dozens of residences for princes of the Ming and Qing dynasties. Taking up nearly 70,000 sq m,. it used to be the residence of Heshen, a high-ranking minister who enjoyed great favor of Emperor Qianlong of the Qing Dynasty. When Emperor Qianlong passed away on Feb 7, 1799, his son, Emperor Jiaqing, stripped Heshen of all his titles and confiscated his belongings, which turned out to be worth some 800 million taels of silver, equaling the national income of a dozen years. Just 15 days later, Heshen was ordered to commit suicide. His residence was granted to Yonglin, or Prince Qingdu. In 1851, Emperor Xianfeng granted the residence to Yixin, or Prince Gong. The building complex is compared to a fairyland and a pearl.

Yonghegong Lamasery

In northeastern Beijing, Yonghegong Lamasery is an important site for Tibetan Buddhism. The temple treasures Buddha niches made of nanmu, a precious wood, and 500 arhats (enlightened disciples of Sakyamuni) carved out of purple sandalwood. The most precious relic in the temple is a giant Buddha statue carved out of a single white sandalwood from Nepal. It took three years to transport the statue from Tibet to Beijing. At 26 m tall and 3 m in diameter, it is the world's biggest wooden Buddha statue.

Beihai Park

Lying to the north of the Forbidden City and to the west of Jingshan Park, Beihai (North Sea) is also an imperial garden. The center of the park is the Jade Island, which has a white pagoda of the Tibetan Buddhism style. The restaurant on the island features imperial cuisine that attracts many visitors from abroad. In winter, the lake is frozen and many people enjoy skating here. The citadel at the southern entrance of the park treasures a jade Buddha statue and a giant jade sculpture of mountain and sea. One can also rent a boat to visit the Nine-Dragon Screen and the Kuaixuetang (Swift Snow Hall).

Jingshan Park

Jingshan, also called Coal Hill, used to be the royal garden to the north of the Forbidden City. In the Yuan Dynasty some 600 years ago, it was a small hill. When Emperor Yongle of the Ming Dynasty ordered the construction of the Forbidden City, the dirt from the city moat was piled onto the small hill. Nicknamed Wansuishan (Hill of 10,000 Years or Hill of the Emperor), the hill was covered in dense vegetation. Emperors liked to escape from the busy work and complex rites to admire flowers, practice shooting arrow, enjoy leisurely banquets and climbing the hill.

Amazing

Zhongnanhai

To the west of the Forbidden City, Zhongnanhai has been the headquarters of the country's central government since the 1910s and off-limits to visitors. It consists of Zhonghai (Middle Sea) formed in the Liao Dynasty (907-1125) and Nanhai (South Sea) built in the Ming Dynasty. It formally became part of the imperial compound in the Qing Dynasty. The front gate of Zhongnanhai is Xinhua (New China) Gate that faces the Chang'an Avenue. Inside the gate is the screen wall printed with Chairman Mao Zedong's handwriting "serving the people".

no!

God of Earth

Temple of Earth

On the eastern side of Andingmen Outer Street, the Temple of Earth is the second major altar of all five imperial altars after the Temple of Heaven. It is the country's biggest altar to pay tribute to earth. Founded in 1530, it is the venue for emperors to pray to the earth for favorable weather and national prosperity. The venue is formed with seven groups of architectures: the Fangzetan Altar, the Earth Deity Hall, the Sacred Warehouse, the Slaughter Pavilion, the Fast Hall, the Sacred Stable and the Bell Tower. The complex reflects traditional Chinese philosophies such as "the sky is round and the earth is square", "the sky is blue and the earth is yellow", "the south belongs to *yin* and the north to *yang*", "dragon and phoenix", "heaven and earth". Its colorful decoration and architectural design are a genius creation of ancient craftsmen.

Agriculture

Altar of the God of Agriculture

At the western side of Andingmen Inner Street, the altar was where emperors worshiped the God of Agriculture, deities of mountains and rivers and others. Remaining architectures include Platform to Observe Farming, Hall of Taisui, Sacred Warehouse, Altar of the God of Agriculture and others.

Temple of Heaven

To the southeast of the Tian'anmen Square, the Temple of Heaven was where the emperors paid tribute to the gods of heaven and earth for good harvests. Founded in 1420, the altar features careful planning, amazing structures and splendid decoration. It is considered as the country's most intricate and beautiful complex of ancient architecture. The treasure in world architecture history is composed of the Hall of Prayer for Good Harvests, the Bridge of Cinnabar Steps (a 360-m-long stone walkway), the Imperial Heavenly Vault, the Altar of Heaven and the Hall of Abstinence.

Temple of Sun

At the northern side of Jianguomen Outer Street, the temple was where emperors worshiped the sun among the five imperial altars. It was also built in 1530.

Temple of Moon

At the western side of Nanlishi Street, the Temple of Moon was first built in 1530 as one of five imperial altars with the Temple of Heaven, Temple of Earth, Temple of Sun and Altar of the Gods of Land and Grain.

Yuanmingyuan

In the northwest of Beijing, Yuanmingyuan was first built in 1709. Covering 3.5 sq km, it was called "Garden of 10,000 Gardens". There used to be 140 architectures in the garden, whose land area was the same as that of the Forbidden City. They gathered the cream of ancient Chinese architecture, horticulture and art. French literary giant Victor Hugo once wrote about Yuanmingyuan which he called "Summer Palace", "Imagine some inexpressible construction, something like a lunar building, and you will have the Summer Palace. Build a dream with marble, jade, bronze and porcelain, frame it with cedar wood, cover it with precious stones, drape it with silk.... Suppose in a word a sort of dazzling cavern of human fantasy with the face of a temple and palace, such was this building." But the British and French troops who invaded Beijing in 1860 set a devastating fire to the imperial garden and looted all the treasures.

Summer Palace

In northwestern Beijing, the Summer Palace is formed with the Wanshou (Longevity) Hill and Kunming Lake. Major sights include the Foxiangge (Pavilion of Buddha's Fragrance), Long Corridor, 17-Hole Bridge and others. Behind the Longevity Hill is the Suzhou Street that models upon the streets of southern China. The architectures in the Summer Palace have a total of some 3,000 rooms. The Long Corridor measures 728 m, with 1,400 colorful paintings telling stories of history and legends. It is the country's longest corridor, winding along the Kunming Lake. Some ancient scholars praised the imperial garden, saying that "although it is built by humans, the garden seems to be created by heavens."

Ming Imperial Tombs

Located on the southern slope of Tianshou Hill in Changping district, the Ming Imperial Tombs are the world's biggest and best preserved imperial cemetery. In an area of 40 sq km, 13 emperors of the Ming Dynasty were buried with 23 empresses and more imperial consorts, princes and princesses. According to the time they were built, the 13 imperial tombs are Changling, Xianling, Jingling, Yuling, Maoling, Tailing, Kangling, Yongling, Zhaoling, Dingling, Qingling, Deling and Siling. The layout of the tombs was modeled upon the Xiaoling tomb in Nanjing of Jiangsu Province, which used to be the capital of Ming Dynasty before Beijing replaced it. Among the 13 tombs, Changling is the grandest, Yongling is the best designed, Siling is the smallest. On the central axis of the cemetery is the 7 km long Sacred Road.

Ruins of the Imperial City Wall

One can find ruins of the imperial city wall in the Ming and Qing dynasties between the Forbidden City and the Wangfujing pedestrian street. At 2.8 km long and 30 m wide, the park has seven sights such as a huge stone carving of ancient Beijing's map and the underground base of the city wall.

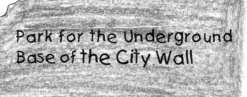

Park for the Underground Base of the City Wall

capital of culture

Museums

China Science & Technology Museum

Situated at the cross of Gulou Outer Street and the northern 3rd Ring Road, this is a comprehensive national museum on science and technology. On exhibition in its dozens of halls are ancient inventions, life, global environment, math, physics and chemistry, engineering and others. Visitors can get a taste of the latest inventions.

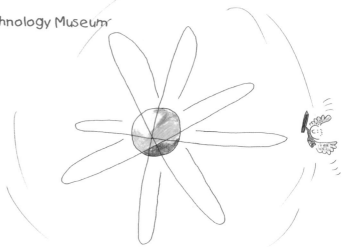

Capital Museum

The Capital Museum has raised the theory of "helping yourself to a touch of history" and here the audience can admire, touch and copy precious cultural relics. The 5,000 items on display are of high cultural value, such as the lacquer table and silk found a few years ago from a tomb of the Han Dynasty (206 BC-AD 220) in Laoshan Hill of western Beijing. In the Cultural Relics Activity Area and the Handy Classroom, visitors can learn to make New Year paintings, pottery, rubbings or ancient coins. The static museum has thus gained dynamic functions.

Dazhongsi Ancient Bell Museum

Lying on the northwestern 3rd Ring Road, the museum is the only one in China displaying ancient bells. First founded in 1733 of the Qing Dynasty, the temple gained the name Big Bell (Dazhong) because of a giant bronze bell left from the time of Emperor Chengzu of the Ming Dynasty. The bell weighs 46 tons and its body is carved with Buddhist inscriptions of 230,000 words in both Chinese and Sanskrit.

China Sports Museum

Lying at No 3 of Anding Street, it collects, displays and studies relics related with sports. On display are ancient Chinese sports, modern Chinese sports, achievements of New China and Olympic medalists. There are some 4,700 relics and 5,000 precious pictures. The museum is an important showcase for the sports culture of China.

Beijing Planetarium

Located to the west of Xizhimen, the Beijing Planetarium is a national science museum. The museum publicizes science knowledge through exhibitions of the Galaxy and other aspects of the universe.

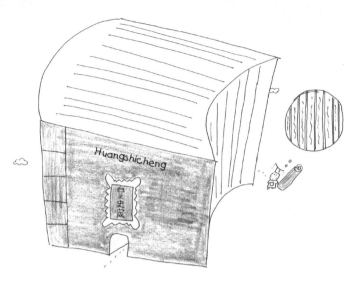

Huang Shi Cheng

Lying to the east of the southern end of Nanchizi Street, the Huang Shi Cheng is an imperial archive of the Ming and Qing dynasties. The words "Huang Shi Cheng" refer to "imperial history stored in a big library". First built in 1543, the architecture's main hall faces south, with its base and walls built with stone slabs. The windows, columns and beams are all made with stones that look like wood, to protect the ancient files from fire and humidity. It has 152 stone containers that treasure the decrees and records of emperors and the imperial family.

China People's Revolution Military Museum

Located on the Fuxing Street, it is the country's only comprehensive museum on military history. It displays major military events, figures and weaponry over the past 5,000 years, as well as the achievements in national defense and People's Liberation Army. The museum has seven halls that display The First Civil War, The Second Civil War, The War of Resistance Against Japanese Aggression, The Third Civil War, weaponry, ancient Chinese wars and modern Chinese wars. There are some 130,000 items, 450,000 historic photos and 100,000 written records.

Beijing Police Museum

Sitting at No 36 of Dongjiaominxiang, the museum is built at the original site of the Beijing branch of the City Bank of the United States. The museum of typical Western architectural style covers 2,000 sq m. It has collected some 7,000 items from home and abroad related with police since the Ming Dynasty. Besides artifacts, the museum also displays photos, illustrations, texts and models. The high technologies in sound, lighting and electricity are perfectly combined with the traditional exhibits.

China Currency Museum

Lying at No 32 of Chengfang Street in Xicheng District, the museum displays the history of money used in China. The five parts talk about the unification of currency, symbolic meaning of ancient coins, silver and golden currency, banks and banknotes, present and future of Chinese currencies. It also holds exhibitions of various themes.

Kaiyuan Tongbao, a coin first issued in Tang Dynasty(AD 618-907).

Beijing Paleozoology Museum

To the west of Beijing Planetarium, the Beijing Paleozoology Museum displays rare fossils of extinct species. The fossil of the giant Mamenchisaurus is 22 m long, and some small dinosaurs are just 1 m long. There are also fossils of fish and bird. The real-life models of dinosaurs, gentle herbivores and toothy carnivores bring audience to prehistoric times. The intact fossil of the giant Yellow River elephant is also displayed here.

Beijing Ancient Observatory

Standing to the southwest of Jianguomen Flyover, the ancient observatory has faithfully recorded the changes of stars and moon for more than 500 years. First built in 1442, it served as the national observatory in Ming and Qing dynasties. On the 14-m high platform are eight astroscopes made in the Qing Dynasty. They have kept the longest record of continuous observation in China. The observatory is famous in the whole world for the intact ancient architecture and equipment.

China Red Sandalwood Museum

The country's biggest private museum on sandalwood furniture is located at No 23, Jianguo Street of Chaoyang District. Sandalwood has always been the most precious and expensive material for Chinese furniture. There are hundreds of furniture dating back to the Ming and Qing dynasties, as well as thousands of imperial art works made of sandalwood, ebony, rock wood, rose wood.

Dabaotai Western Han Dynasty Tomb Museum

This is a little known but very interesting museum built on the underground mausoleum of Liu Jian (73-45 BC), a prince of the Western Han Dynasty (206 BC-AD 25). Covering 18,000 sq m, it attracts viewers' full attention with well-preserved remains of the tomb owners and sacrificial animals. There are also exhibitions on the structures of ancient Chinese emperors' mausoleums.

Beijing Museum of Natural History

Lying on Tianqiao South Street, the museum is the first one on natural science built after the founding of New China. It displays animals, plants, extinct species and dinosaurs. It is a world leader in terms of intact fossils of major ancient mammals.

China Folk Opera Museum

The museum is located inside the Huguang Guild of Hufangqiao, a famous venue for Peking Opera shows. The main part of the exhibition features the history of folk operas in Beijing with precious documents, relics, pictures and audio-visual files. Visitors can find the picture showing Peking Opera master Mei Lanfang finding his teacher and the costume once used by Yang Xiaolou, a Peking Opera master in the role of generals.

China Arts and Crafts Museum

Lying at the northeastern corner of the Fuxingmen Flyover, it is the country's first national museum on arts and crafts. Visitors can find the cream of Chinese arts and crafts such as jadeware, ivory, wood carving, stone carving, ceramics, lacquerware, embroidery, drawnwork, cloisonné, gold and silver ware, inlaid, tinware and copperware. There are also four large-scale jadeite works that are listed as national treasures.

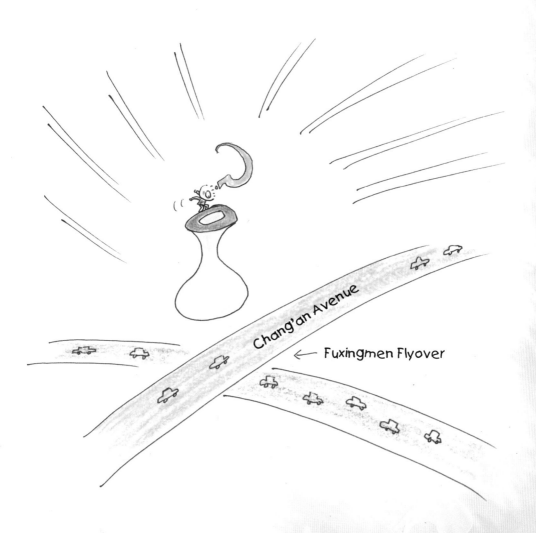

Chang'an Avenue

← Fuxingmen Flyover

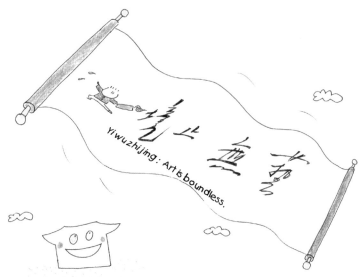

Yiwuzhijing: Art is boundless.

Beijing Arts Museum

Located in the imperial Wanshou Temple founded in 1577 on the western 3rd Ring Road, the museum is nicknamed Small Forbidden City in Western Beijing. It boasts a collection of some 50,000 precious items from the primitive society to the Qing Dynasty. Main exhibits include calligraphy, paintings, rubbings, letters, embroidery, ceramics, furniture, coins, imperial seals and others. There are some 100,000 ancient books from the Song Dynasty (960-1279) till the Republic of China (1912-1949).

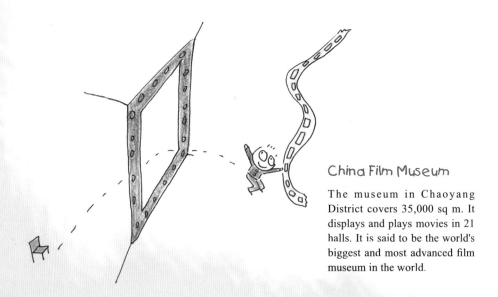

China Film Museum

The museum in Chaoyang District covers 35,000 sq m. It displays and plays movies in 21 halls. It is said to be the world's biggest and most advanced film museum in the world.

Memorial of the War of Resistance Against Japanese Aggression

The memorial is located in the former Wanping County near the Lugou (Marco Polo) Bridge where the July 7 Incident occurred in 1937 to mark the beginning of the War of Resistance Against Japanese Aggression (1937-1945). The memorial displays the happenings of the war, atrocities of Japanese invaders, the Chinese people's heroic fight against the invaders and national heroes. There is also a gallery that brings the July 7 Incident alive through modern technology. There are some 3,800 photos and files, as well as 5,000 artifacts.

Museum of City Wall in Liao and Jin Dynasties

Located inside the Yulin Community outside You'anmen, it is built on the site of a watergate on the city wall of Zhongdu (the name of Beijing) in the Jin Dynasty (1115-1234). Covering 2,500 sq m, the museum has an underground exhibition hall that covers the watergate. Built with rock and wood, the gate is 43.4 m long. The culvert where water used to pass through is 21 m long and 7.7 m broad. It is the biggest ancient watergate found in China. The museum displays the history and layout of Beijing before, during and after the Liao (907-1125) and Jin dynasties.

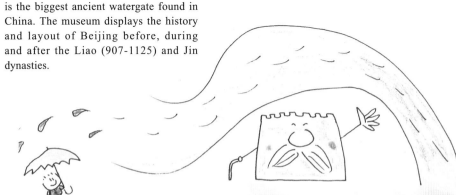

National Museum of Modern Chinese Literature

At No 45 of Wenxueguan Street in Chaoyang District, the building is an icon of contemporary Chinese literature. There are some 380,000 items, including 13,824 manuscripts. It houses 81 specialized collections of the works by Ba Jin, Bing Xin and other famous literary masters.

Peking Man Site at Zhoukoudian

Built in a cave of Longgu Hill in Zhoukoudian of Fangshan District, the site preserves the world's richest findings in paleoanthropology. The skull of Peking Man and the evidence of using fire have contributed greatly to the study of early human evolution. The site includes a museum of the Peking Man, the Ape-Man Cave and other galleries.

National Air and Space Museum

At Donggaodi of Fengtai District, the museum showcases latest development of Chinese astronautic technology. Besides the main hall, there are also halls to display high technology and special technology. Visitors can find the "Long March" series of rockets and satellites of Fengyun and Dongfanghong series.

Ruins of Yan Capital of Western Zhou Dynasty

Covering some 6 sq km in the Dongjialin Village of Liulihe Town, Fangshan District, it is an important site of the capital of the Dukedom of Yan during the Western Zhou Dynasty (11th c. -771 BC). Visitors can find traces of Beijing's early history as the first city was constructed some 3,000 years ago.

Cultural tour

Wangfujing Paleoanthropology Site

Lying at the passage from the New Oriental Plaza to the subway, the site is at the busiest commercial center of Beijing. It is the first time such an important site for paleoanthropology was discovered at the center of a cosmopolis. At about 12 m deep underground, the site can be dated back to some 25,000 years ago and show how ancient humans once lived in the area.

Shichahai

Acknowledged as one of five most beautiful urban compounds in the country, Shichahai is a perfect blend of old and new. At the Di'anmen West Street, Shichahai has preserved the strongest flavors of folk Beijing life. There are many old Beijing residents dwelling in the *hutong* alleys where visitors can find residences of celebrities and grand courtyards of nobles in the Ming and Qing dynasties.

Guanghua Temple

At No 31 of the Ya'er Hutong on the northern bank of Houhai Lake, the temple is also the site of Beijing Buddhism Association. It is said that a Buddhist master of the Yuan Dynasty (1206-1368) begged alms to build the temple. Upon the 1st and 15th days of each lunar month, the temple holds some religious ceremonies. At every Saturday, the Beijing Buddhist Music Troupe gives a performance here. Upon the 8th day of the last lunar month, the temple prepares porridge and distributes it among local residents. The tradition has lasted for centuries.

广化寺

Guanghua
Temple

Imperial College

Guozijian, or Imperial College, was the highest educational administration in Yuan, Ming and Qing dynasties. Built at the Chengxian Street in 1306, the college has three layers of courtyards where the buildings are perfectly symmetrical along the central axis. The college used to teach rites, music, law, archery, horsemanship, calligraphy and maths. It was the ideal and pride of all ancient Chinese scholars to enter the college.

Confucius Temple

Near the Imperial College at the Guozijian Street, the Confucius Temple is the second largest memorial to Confucius after the Confucius Temple in Qufu of Shandong Province. Ceremonies were held at the Dacheng (Great Achievements) Hall to pay tribute to Confucius in the Yuan, Ming and Qing dynasties. First founded in 1302, the temple has 198 stone tablets bearing all the names of *jinshi* — scholars who passed the highest-level imperial civil service examinations — in the three dynasties.

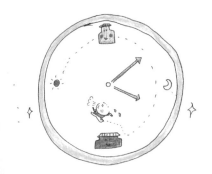

Drum and Bell Towers

At the Di'anmen Outer Street, the towers were first installed in 1420 to announce the time to the whole city. The Drum Tower was the center of time for the capital of Qing Dynasty. About 100 m to its north is the Bell Tower, where the huge bronze bell is considered one of the biggest of its kind in China.

Lugou (Marco Polo) Bridge

Built on the Yongding River in southwestern Beijing in 1189 of the Jin Dynasty, the bridge is the oldest remaining stone arch bridge in the city. Explorer Marco Polo (c. 1254-1324) of Venice, Italy, described the bridge in his writing and it is assumed that he visited it during his 16 years of stay in China. The moon above the bridge at daybreak was once regarded as one of eight most enchanted sights of the ancient capital. At the time when it was built, the pier near the bridge was a major gateway for Beijing. There are 498 stone lions of different shapes on the columns and decorative boards. Locals love to quote an idiom that says the lions on Lugou Bridge are impossible to count.

Deshengmen Embrasured Watchtower

To the north of the western sea of Shichahai, the watchtower was built in 1439 of the Ming Dynasty. It is one of the best-preserved embrasured watchtowers in Beijing. Deshengmen was where the imperial troops set out to battle, and its name symbolizes victory.

Kublai Khan

White Pagoda Temple

The temple in Xicheng District was founded in 1271 and its site was chosen by Kublai Khan himself. The 50-m-tall white pagoda in the temple took eight years to build. It is one of the country's oldest and biggest remaining pagodas of Tibetan Buddhism. The pagoda is an important landmark for Dadu, name of Beijing as the Grand Capital of Yuan Dynasty.

Dongyue Temple

At the Chaoyangmen Outer Street, this is the biggest Taoist temple in northern China and features folk culture. First built in the early Yuan Dynasty, it enshrines the

God of Mount Taishan. The temple has 376 rooms. Outside the front gate is a green glazed archway. It is said that the calligraphy on the archway was written by Yan Song, a cruel imperial minister of the Ming Dynasty. There are some 3,000 sculptures of various deities in Taoism and folklore. It is said the sculptures of Dongyue Temple are the best of its kind in the country.

Guangji Temple

At No 25, Fuchengmen Inner Street, the temple is the site of China Buddhism Association and the center of the country's Buddhist activities. First built in the Jin Dynasty (1115-1234), the temple is known for strict doctrines. In its western part is a three-story white marble altar where novices are initiated into monkhood.

Five Pagodas Temple

On the northern bank of the Changhe River to the east of Baishiqiao outside Xizhimen, the temple preserves the country's oldest and most intact pagodas with Buddha's warrior attendants on the base. Indian Buddhist master Panditarama had many pleasant talks with Zhu Di (1360-1424), or Emperor Chengzu of Ming Dynasty. The emperor conferred him the title of "State Tutor" and granted him the place to build Zhenjue Temple. As there are five pagodas in the temple, it is commonly known as Wuta (Five Pagodas) Temple. The "Forest of Stone Carvings in Beijing" displayed inside and outside halls present a comprehensive history of stone carving in the city.

Wangfujing Catholic Church

The Catholic church is located to the east of the Wangfujing pedestrian street. The small square in front of the church has become a favorite choice of newly weds to take their wedding pictures.

White Cloud Temple

Baiyunguan Temple

Outside the Xibianmen Gate, it is Beijing's biggest Taoist temple and one of the country's best preserved Taoist sites. Baiyunguan is one of three original temples for the Quanzhen Sect of Taoism. The Chinese Taoist Association is located here. First built in AD 739 of the Tang Dynasty (AD 618-907), the temple is formed with four huge courtyards. Its name means "White Cloud Temple".

Niujie Street

On the eastern side of the middle of Niujie Street is the Niujie Mosque, the biggest and oldest Islamic mosque in Beijing. Dating back to AD 996 of the Liao Dynasty, the mosque of wooden structure features striking Islamic decorations. There are two tombstones bearing Arabic inscriptions made in the 13th century. Another stone tablet dating back to 1496 of the Ming Dynasty carries Chinese and Arabic inscriptions about the founding of the mosque. They provide precious information for studying the history of Islam in China.

Tianqiao

Tianqiao is a general name for the area in the middle of Andingmen Inner Street of Xuanwu District. In history, the Tianqiao Fair was very popular among the local residents, who thronged there for various kinds of recreation and commodities.

Tianqiao Feat

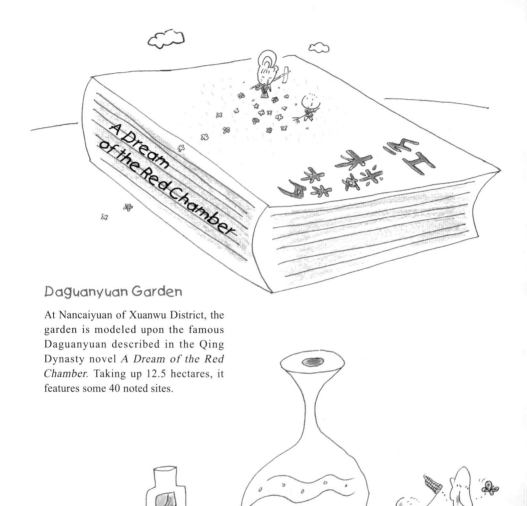

Daguanyuan Garden

At Nancaiyuan of Xuanwu District, the garden is modeled upon the famous Daguanyuan described in the Qing Dynasty novel *A Dream of the Red Chamber*. Taking up 12.5 hectares, it features some 40 noted sites.

Baoguo Temple

Located on the northern side of Guang'anmen Inner Street, the temple was first built in the Liao Dynasty but collapsed in the early Ming Dynasty. In 1466, it was rebuilt and named Ci'en Temple. Local people call it Baoguo (Patriotism) Temple. It has become a market of antiques.

Lingshan Hill

Standing at 2,302 m above sea level, Lingshan is the highest mountain in Beijing. It has the biggest alpine meadow in the capital. But the local weather changes frequently. While it is sunny at the foot of the mountain, one might encounter a thunderstorm on the way to the mountain top. It is nicknamed Small Tibet for its height and cool weather. At 122 km away from downtown Beijing, the mountain is located at Qingshui Town of Mentougou District, bordering Zhuolu County of Hebei Province.

Site of City Wall for Yuan Capital Dadu

To the north of Xizhimen, visitors can find an earthen mound marked as the site of city wall for Dadu, the name of Beijing as the capital of Yuan Dynasty. The city wall, gate and other architectures no longer exist. But a narrow strip of garden lies from Mingguangcun crossroad to Guangmingqiao crossroad. In the past, the area was sheltered by giant trees and fog often lingered over the woods. It was one of the eight famous sights in Beijing.

Badachu

Lying on the southern slope of the Western Mountain, the famous site gained the name because of eight temples: Chang'an Temple, Lingguang Temple, Sanshan Nunnery, Dabei Temple, Longquan Nunnery, Xiangjie Temple, Baozhu Cave and Zhengguo Temple. The natural landscape and profound religious culture draw numerous visitors everyday.

Tanzhe Temple

In southeastern Mentougou District, the temple was built more than 1,000 years ago. Locals often say that Beijing was built after the Tanzhe Temple. There are many pagodas and mountain streams. Every year, when magnolia bursts into blossom, the fragrance permeates the air. There are many giant trees in the mountain where the temple is located.

Jietai Temple

Also in Mentougou District, the temple is the highest academy for Buddhism in China. "*Jie*" means religious commandments, and "*jie tai*" refers to the altar where people are initiated into monkhood or nunhood. The white marble altar in the temple is carved with 113 niches. A statue of Sakyamuni sits on the lotus base on the altar. The ceiling above the altar is painted with golden dragons. The larger altar in the open field is where highest level ceremonies are held.

commandment

Miaofeng Mountain

Also located in Mentougou District, Miaofeng Mountain is shaped like a lotus flower. Since the rule of Emperor Chongzhen in the Ming Dynasty, an annual fair has been held in the temple at the top of the mountain. There are vast fields of rose at the foot of the mountain, bringing fragrance to the whole area.

Cuandixia Village

At Zhaitang of Mentougou District, the village has the biggest number of *siheyuan* courtyards of the Ming and Qing dynasties among villages in the suburbs of Beijing. The village is built along the northern slope of a valley. There are some 600 rooms in about 70 courtyards. As it is located below Cuanli'ankou, a military pass built in the Ming Dynasty, the village is named Cuandixia (Below Cuan) — "*cuan*" means to cook food over fire. For centuries, the village has been an important stop on the northwestern post road.

Cuan:
to cook food over fire.

Fragrant Hill

On the eastern slope of the Western Mountain, the Fragrant Hill is covered with smoke tree that turns crimson in autumn. The Biyun (Green Cloud) and Wofo (Reclining Buddha) temples are two famous Buddhist sites. The Shuangqing Villa was the residence of Mao Zedong before the founding of New China.

Peking and Tsinghua universities

The two universities are known in the world for their long history and high academic level.

Peking University used to be named Jingshi Grand Academy and changed to the present name in 1912. Cai Yuanpei (1868-1940) is the most famous president in the university's history. It was he who championed the idea of "following freedom of thoughts and absorbing the cream of cultures". Entering the southern gate and walking northward, one will find the Peking University Centennial Memorial Hall and library. Further north are the Boya Pagoda and Weiming Lake, where lies the spirit and soul of Peking University. The lakeside wood shelters the tomb of American journalist and author Edgar Snow (1905-1972), the statue of Cai Yuanpei and a tablet carved with a poem by Emperor Qianlong. From the western gate, one can follow the streams to find the tomb of American geologist Amadeus William Grabau (1870-1946), the statue of Spanish writer Miguel de Cervantes Saavedra (1547-1616) and the memorial tablet for the South-West Associated University formed by combining Peking, Tsinghua and Nankai universities during the War of Resistance Against Japanese Aggression (1937-1945).

On the other side of the street lies the Tsinghua University. Starting from the Gongzi Hall, the Tsinghua University is centered on the majestic auditorium that symbolizes the spirit of the university. Zhu Ziqing (1898-1948), a famous scholar, once wrote a prose titled *Moonlit Lotus Pond (Hetang Yuese)* on his musings over the lotus pond in the Jinchun Garden of Tsinghua University. The famous garden was also a residence for Emperor Xianfeng of Qing Dynasty. There are two pavilions on the wooded hill behind the Gongzi Hall. The pavilions carry the title of "Shui Mu Nian Hua" (Years of Water and Wood). It is the best-known symbol of the university.

Hongluo Temple

Lying in Huairou District, the temple is the biggest Buddhist site in northern Beijing. First built in Eastern Jin Dynasty (AD 317-420), it was expanded in Tang Dynasty (AD 618-907). For centuries, it has been a sacred site of Buddhism, cultivating many reverend masters. It commands the same high status in Buddhism as the Putuo Island of Zhejiang Province. There are three unique natural sights at the temple: the bamboo grove, the male and female gingko trees, the ivy climbing on a giant pine. The broadleaf forest covers 300 hectares. Every October, the Hongluo Mountain puts on a brilliant dress. Visitors can take the cableway to reach the mountain top and get a bird's-eye view.

Yunju Temple

The temple in Fangshan District has three kinds of precious Buddhist scriptures written, printed or carved on paper, wood and rock. During the Sui, Tang, Liao, Jin, Yuan and Ming dynasties from the 6th to the 17th centuries, Buddhist scriptures were printed from the stone boards in the temple. To protect the stone boards from sun and rain, they were moved into an underground chamber and nine caves of the Shijing (Stone Scripture) Mountain. The temple has some 2,000 hand-written and printed scriptures dating back to the Ming Dynasty. One of the scriptures was written by Reverend Zuhui of the Miaolian Temple, who cut his own tongue to use the blood as ink.

Exhibition venues

Beijing Exhibition Center

Built in 1954, it is the first major comprehensive exhibition center in Beijing. Chairman Mao Zedong wrote the name for the center and Premier Zhou Enlai cut the ribbon at its opening ceremony. Located at the commercial center of Xizhimen, it has the exhibition hall, Beijing Exhibition Center Theater and Moscow Restaurant.

National Art Museum of China

Built at the Wusi Street, the museum is the biggest and highest-level art gallery in the country. It records the history of Chinese fine arts and introduces latest trends in the world to China.

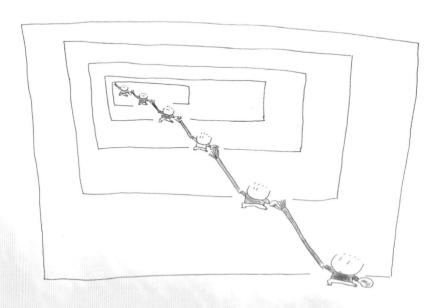

National Agriculture Exhibition Center

Built in 1959, it faces the embassy area on the eastern side of the 3rd Ring Road. There are dozens of hotels and restaurants near the center. It is the only large-scale garden-style exhibition center in the country and features typical Chinese architectural style. Covering 52 hectares, it is densely wooded and various blossoms enchant visitors for most part of the year.

International Exhibition Center

Located at Jing'anzhuang of northern 3rd Ring Road, it is one of the biggest modern exhibition centers in the country. With an exhibition capacity of 170,000 sq m, it has seven halls, among which the Number One hall covers more than 50,000 sq m.

Fayuan Temple

At the southern end of Jiaozi Hutong of the Fayuansiqian Street, it is the oldest existing temple in downtown Beijing. Emperor Taizong, founder of Tang Dynasty, ordered the construction of the Minzhong Temple in AD 645. In 1734, Emperor Yongzheng of Qing Dynasty expanded the temple and renamed it Fayuan — Source of Buddhist Law. The China Buddhism College and China Buddhism Books and Cultural Relics Library are located in the temple. The Minzhong Mansion built in the Tang Dynasty collapsed before the 14th century. There are some broken stone tablets belonging to the original Minzhong Temple.

Cultural Palace of Nationalities

Lying on the northern side of Fuxingmen Inner Street, the architecture features strong ethnic style. Many exhibitions about the 56 nationalities of China are held at the exhibition hall, library and museum in the building.

Libraries

National Library of China

At Zhongguancun South Street of Haidian District, the library has collected some 20 million volumes in its 19 stories above ground and three stories underground, which have a total floor area of 60,000 sq m. Listed as one of the world's ten biggest libraries, it has 46 reading rooms on different focuses, attracting nearly 10,000 readers everyday. The national library's new building opened to the public in Sep 2008, increasing the library's total floor space to 250,000 sq m, making it the world's third largest library. The new building displays ancient books and provides readers with wireless access to the Internet besides many other latest technologies.

Residences of celebrities

Former Residence of Soong Ching Ling

Taking up 20,000 sq m at No 46 of the northern rim of Houhai Lake, it is the largest residence of a celebrity in Beijing. Madame Soong Ching Ling (1893-1981) was the wife of Dr Sun Yat-Sen, Father of the Republic of China. She lived here from 1963 till May 29, 1981, when she passed away at 88. She established a foundation for children's education.

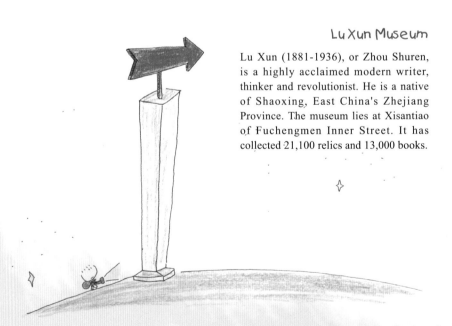

Lu Xun Museum

Lu Xun (1881-1936), or Zhou Shuren, is a highly acclaimed modern writer, thinker and revolutionist. He is a native of Shaoxing, East China's Zhejiang Province. The museum lies at Xisantiao of Fuchengmen Inner Street. It has collected 21,100 relics and 13,000 books.

Residence of Lao She

Lao She (1899-1966) is the penname of Shu Qingchun, one of the most important modern writers of China whose writing focused on the common people of old Beijing. His residence is at the No 19 courtyard of Fengfu Hutong, Dengshikou West Street. It displays the works and life of Lao She.

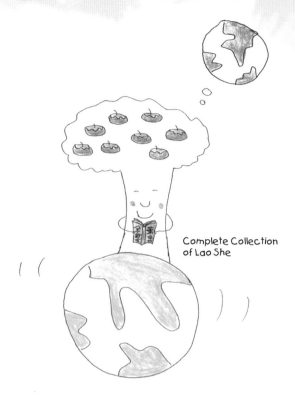

Complete Collection of Lao She

Residence of Mao Dun

The small courtyard of typical Beijing style at No 13, Houyuan'ensi Hutong, Jiaodaokou South Street was home to famous writer Mao Dun in the last few years of his life. Mao Dun (1896-1981) is the penname of Shen Dehong, who also styled himself Yanbing. He had been the Cultural Minister of China and Chairman of China Writers' Association.

Residence of Guo Moruo

The courtyard at No 18 of Qianhai West Street to the west of Shichahai Lake used to be part of the Residence of Prince Gong and takes up 7,000 sq m. From 1963, Guo Moruo (1892-1978) spent the last 15 years of his life at the well-maintained courtyard. He has been lauded as the country's most famous writer, playwright, poet, archaeologist, expert of ancient Chinese written characters and social activist.

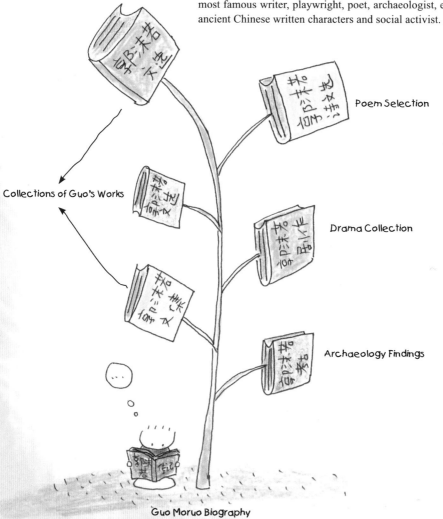

Poem Selection

Collections of Guo's Works

Drama Collection

Archaeology Findings

Guo Moruo Biography

Memorial of Xu Beihong

Xu Beihong (1895-1953) was one of the country's most important modern painters and art educators. He successfully combined the skills of traditional Chinese painting with Western arts. His works, especially those on horses, feature great skills. The memorial was relocated from Shoulu Street of Dongcheng District to Xinjiekou North Street. It displays the life, works and collection of the painter.

Memorial of Guo Shoujing

Guo Shoujing (1231-1316), an astronomer and expert of water conservancy, once lived at the Huitong Memorial on the northern rim of Xihai Lake, presiding over the water conservancy work of the whole country. Old Beijing's complex waterway system was accomplished under his instruction. The memorial was refurnished during the rule of Emperor Qianlong (1711-1799) in the Qing Dynasty. The elegant building complex has three exhibition rooms to display Guo's achievements.

Memorial of Cao Xueqin

Cao Xueqin (1724-1764) is known for his classic novel *A Dream of the Red Chamber* depicting a declining noble family's life in the mid-Qing Dynasty. The descendant of a high-ranking official spent most of his life in poverty. At the Fragrant Hill of Beijing's western suburbs, he spent ten years working on the great novel. The memorial is located at No 39, Zhengbaiqi of Fragrant Hill.

A Dream of the Red Chamber

Memorial of Mei Lanfang

Mei Lanfang (1894-1961) is the best-known master of Peking Opera specializing in young female role. The memorial is built in a courtyard on Huguosi Street of Xicheng District, where Mei Lanfang once resided for ten years. It houses some 30,000 items like letters, paintings, calligraphy works, manuscripts and costumes. There are some invaluable photos showing Mei Lanfang with famous Chinese and foreign actors and dramatists. Also on display are the performance program lists that Mei staged in his life.

Residence of Cheng Yanqiu

Cheng Yanqiu (1904-1958) was one of four most prominent actors in the *danjue* (young female) role of Peking Opera. He debuted at the age of 11 and created the Cheng School which still enjoys a large following. His residence at No 39, Xisi Beisantiao is a courtyard covering 390 sq m.

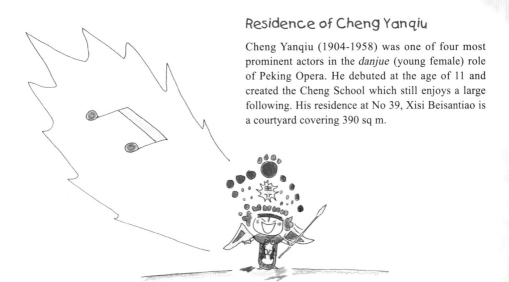

Memorial of Wen Tianxiang

Wen Tianxiang (1236-1282) was an imperial minister of the Southern Song Dynasty (1127-1279) who fought the invasion of Mongolians heroically. The memorial at No 63, Fuxue Hutong, Dongcheng District, was built on the basis of a prison where Wen Tianxiang was once kept for three tormenting years before he was executed by Kublai Khan. In Ming and Qing dynasties, sacrificial ceremonies were held here to commemorate the national hero. The memorial still maintains the ancient architectural style and covers 600 sq m. There are several stone tablets engraved with the life story and portrait of Wen Tianxiang, dating back to the Ming and Qing times.

Ten landmarks of Beijing

1950s

- Great Hall of the People
- Museum of Chinese History and Museum of Chinese Revolution
- China People's Revolutionary Military Museum
- National Agriculture Exhibition Center
- Beijing Railway Station
- Workers' Stadium
- Cultural Palace of Nationalities
- Hotel of Nationalities
- Diaoyutai State Guesthouse
- Prime Hotel

1980s

- New Building of the Beijing Library
- International Exhibition Center
- China Central Television
- Capital Airport Terminal
- Beijing International Hotel
- Daguanyuan Park
- Beijing Great Wall Sheraton Hotel
- China Grand Theater
- Memorial of the War of Resistance Against Japanese Aggression
- Dongsishitiao Subway Station

1990s

O Central Radio and TV Tower
O Olympic Sports Center and Asian Games Village
O Beijing New World Center
O Green House of Beijing Botanical Garden
O New Building of Capital Library
O New Building of Tsinghua University Library
O Foreign Languages Teaching and Research Press
O Beijing Henderson Center
O New Oriental Plaza
O Beijing International Finance Building

21st century

O Bird Nest
O Water Cube
O CCTV new building
O National Center for the Performing Arts
O China Millennium Monument
O Capital Museum
O Xihuan Plaza
O Terminal 3 of Beijing International Airport
O New Beijing Planetarium
O China World Trade Center Phase 3

Bird Nest

The National Stadium is better known as "Bird Nest" because of its shape. Lying in the southern part of the Olympic Park, it was the main venue of the 2008 29th Olympic Games held in Beijing. On a total land area of 21 hectares, the architecture takes up 258,000 sq m. The stadium has 91,000 seats, among which 11,000 are temporary. The opening and closing ceremonies of the Olympic Games and Paralympics were held here. Track and field events, as well as the football finals were also held at the Bird Nest. After the Olympics, the Olympic heritage is becoming a landmark with comprehensive functions in sports, shopping, eatery, recreation, exhibition and other activities.

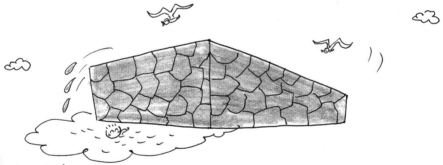

Water Cube

The National Aquatics Center is nick-named "Water Cube" due to its appearance. The building is covered with two layers of plastic films between which are 3,065 inflated blue bubbles. Under different lighting, the bubbles have a dreamy appearance and help strengthen the architecture. The Olympic landmark witnessed the birth of all swimming medals in the Beijing Olympic Games. The Water Cube and the Bird Nest lie on the west and east of the capital's central axis, putting a modern touch to the ancient city.

CCTV new building

Part of the new building for China Central Television (CCTV) entered operation before the Beijing Olympics and many sports events were broadcast here. The complex looks like a "Z" from the air. The two supporting buildings tilt slightly as if defying gravity. The main building is where the programs are produced; while the auxiliary building is open to the public with a hotel, digital theater, multi-functional hall, studio, conference hall and cafeteria. Visitors can enter the first underground floor from the entrance near the Eastern 3rd Ring Road, look at the studios, then take the lift to the 37th floor, go through the souvenir shop and reach the public hall. There are three observation posts with glass floors at the protruding corner of the mid-air corridor, allowing visitors a bird's-eye view of the city. Climbing by the stairs to the 38th floor, one can take the lift down to the underground exit.

Capital Museum

The museum with modern equipment lies to the west of Baiyun Street in Xicheng District. Among its 250,000 collected items are bronze ware, ceramics, paintings and calligraphy, stone carvings, currency, jade ware, seals, embroidery, Buddhist statues, treasures of ancient scholars, art works of bamboo, wood, ivory and antler, as well as folk artifacts. There are quite a number of precious works which are the only one of a kind in the whole world.

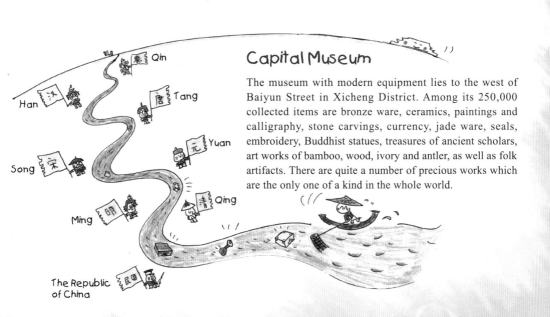

Xihuan Plaza

Lying to the northwest of the Xizhimen Flyover in Xicheng District, the plaza is composed of a multifunctional transportation hubbub, a six-floor commercial center, three office buildings that soar nearly 100 m into the air and a 60-m tall comprehensive building. With a total floor space of 260,000 sq m, the plaza is the biggest building complex to the west of Beijing's central axis. The entire complex is majestic and elegant, with the main buildings shaped like ships ready to embark on a distant journey.

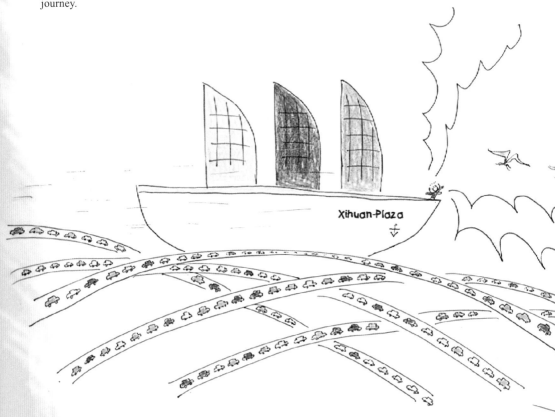

Xihuan-Plaza

Terminal 3 of Beijing International Airport

The world's biggest single airport terminal took four years and an astronomical 27 billion yuan to complete and it entered full operation on Feb 29, 2008. Measuring 2,900 m long from north to south, 790 m broad and 45 m tall, the terminal, better known as T3, covers a total floor space of 986,000 sq m. Looking like a giant dragon, T3 opened a new national gate for Beijing before the Olympics was held.

New Beijing Planetarium

At No 138 of Xiwai Street, Xicheng District, the new planetarium neighbors the old planetarium and has seven floors, among which two are underground. The designers made the planetarium a giant stage of the Theory of Relativity, the String Theory and other theories of modern astrophysics. The new planetarium can be seen as an epitome of the universe. Looking from the north, the architecture appears like a transparent glass box, with a 30-m glass screen that bends gently near the dome of the old planetarium. At the main entrance, the screen bends into a tunnel that reminds visitors of the "wormhole" through which one could travel to other spaces and times. The new planetarium has the SGI Digital Space Theater, the 3D Popular Science Theater, the 4D Popular Science Theater, the Solar Observatory, the Public Observatory, an exhibition hall for solar science, a laboratory of astronomical science, an information center for the public, a public reading room and a library.

New Beijing Planetarium

China World Trade Center Phase 3

The third phase of the China World Trade Center has a total investment of $800 million and takes up 6.27 hectares between the Eastern 3rd Ring Road and the Guanghua Street. With a floor space of 540,000 sq m, it will form an enormous building complex of 1.1 million sq m with the first and second phases of the China World Trade Center to become the world's biggest international trade center. With 75 floors, the building will be 330 m tall, making it the highest skyscraper in Beijing. Besides a super 5 star hotel, office building, international top-end shops, movie theater and other facilities, the complex will include Beijing's biggest banquet hall that spans over 10,000 sq m. The building complex will be a landmark of Beijing beyond the commercial landscape.

He who fails to reach the Great Wall is not a man.

Badaling

In Yanqing District, the Badaling section of the Great Wall winds along gorgeous mountains like a giant dragon. This section is the most frequently visited part of the Great Wall with convenient transportation and fantastic view. There are many beacon towers, defense towers and a citadel to fend off enemies. From the citadel to the highest point — Northern 8th Tower, the popular northern route is 1.5 km long.

Juyong Pass

The crucial pass on the Great Wall lies in Changping District. In the Ming Dynasty, great efforts were made to enhance the defense system at Juyong Pass. From north to south, the defense consists of a northern entrance, the Juyong Outer Town (which is Badaling), the Upper Pass, the Middle Pass (known as Juyong Pass) and the southern entrance. Juyong Pass was the headquarters of the troops garrisoned here. Helmet, armor, spear, bow, arrow, firearm and other weaponry were stored at the pass, whose architecture shows many aspects of Chinese culture.

Mutianyu

At 25 km away from Huairou Town, Mutianyu is the biggest section of the Great Wall that was built with the highest quality. Xu Da, a general under Zhu Yuanzhang who founded the Ming Dynasty in 1368, presided over the construction of Mutianyu section. Built on the basis of an older Wall dating back to the Northern Qi Dynasty (AD 550-577), the section is 2,250 m long with 22 defense towers.

Simatai

Founded in 1368 of the Ming Dynasty in Beikou Town of northeastern Miyun District, Simatai is built on the most perilous mountains among the unconnected sections of the Great Wall that came into form over thousands of years. Qi Jiguang and Tan Lun, two famous patriotic generals of the Ming Dynasty, enhanced the defense work in the 16th century. There are 16 defense towers on the eastern part of the section.

Yanhecheng

Yanhecheng was a small town built with pebbles in Mentougou District of western Beijing. With its back on the Lingshan Mountain and facing the Yongding River, the town, which is also a part of the Great Wall defense work, controlled traffic both on land and on water. Its layout is carefully designed to suit the defense purposes.

Jinshanling

Bordering Miyun District and Luanping County of Hebei Province, Jinshanling section is the most representative part of the Great Wall built in the Ming Dynasty. General Xu Da presided over its construction in 1368. Qi Jiguang and Tan Lun, who fought against Japanese invaders, enhanced and expanded the section in 1567. The national scenic area has been listed as a World Cultural Heritage Site.

Jiankou and Jiuyanlou

Jiankou is a section of the Great Wall that looks like a curving bow. It is one of the most dangerous parts of the Ming Dynasty Great Wall, located in Badaohe Township of Huairou District. Jiuyanlou Defense Tower is built at the Huoyan (Flame) Mountain bordering Yanqi Town of Huairou District and Sihai Town of Yanqing District. It is 155 m higher than the Wangjing Tower of Simatai section of the Great Wall. The two-storeyed square building is the biggest defense tower with the biggest number of observation posts on the entire Great Wall. Of all the defense towers, this is the most important as it sits on the conjuncture of the inner and outer parts of the Great Wall.

Gubeikou

Gubeikou lies on the southern slopes of Panlong (Reclining Dragon) and Wohu (Crouching Tiger) mountains in the Yanshan Mountain Range of northeastern Miyun District. The Chaohe River flows into the Miyun Reservoir from the northern entrance of the valley. Situated between Shanhai and Juyong passes, the Gubeikou section of the Great Wall is less than 100 km away from downtown Beijing. It has been a defense pivot for the capital since ancient times. With many historic sites and natural scenery spots, the valley was the vital passage for Qing emperors to go on hunting and inspection tours, and hold sacrificial ceremonies for their ancestors in Northeast China. At the military camp here, Emperor Kangxi once stayed during the summer and Emperor Qianlong once inspected the troops.

Charming views over here

Beijing Botanical Garden

Covering 400 hectares, the garden is close to the Fragrant Hill. It has some 560,000 plants of 5,000 species. The plants exhibition garden has 11 sections displaying magnolia, *mei* blossom, Chinese flowering crab-apple and other plants. The Wofo (Reclining Buddha) Temple, the tomb of revolutionist Liang Qichao (1873-1929) and Memorial of Cao Xueqin are also located in the garden that has a nature reserve and scientific research area.

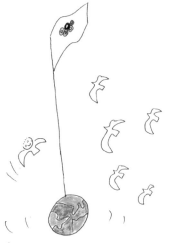

Wow! waterfall!

Olympic Park

Lying on the northern end of the central axis of Beijing, the Olympic Park is specially designed and built for the 2008 Olympic Games in Beijing. Taking up 1,200 hectares, it has 15 halls and centers for matches and training sessions. The main stadium has a capacity of 80,000 seats. There are also the Beijing International Exhibition and Sports center, two comprehensive stadiums and the athlete village. The forests and meadows cover 760 hectares. Twelve major games were held here during the 2008 Olympics. The park has become a center of sports, exhibition, culture and recreation after the Olympics.

Yanqi Lake

The lake gained the name Yanqi (Habitat of Wild Geese) as many wild geese come here to breed in spring. The lake at the foot of the Yanshan Mountain about 8 km to the north of Huaiyou District is surrounded by recreational facilities. One can enjoy rocket bungee-jumping, parachuting on water and water screen movie among other things.

No. 1 Waterfall in Eastern Beijing

At a fall of 200 m, the waterfall in northeastern Miyun District boasts of the biggest volume of water in the capital's suburbs. Among the 10 major pools, the biggest is called the Blue Dragon Pool.

Chinese Ethnic Culture Park

Lying to the southwest of the Asian Games Village, the park is a museum of all 56 ethnic groups of China. All the 56 ethnic villages in the southern and northern parts of the park are built at the real size. The cottages, houses, pagodas and bridges among hills and streams provide visitors with glimpses of the ethnic cultures. Many performance troupes from remote areas stage live shows for visitors.

Longtanhu Park

Inside Zuo'anmen Gate of Chongwen District, the park features the culture of dragon, a symbol of the Chinese nation. Besides the Longtan (Dragon Pool) Lake, the park is also known for the Longyin (Dragon Roar) Mansion. The Dragon Stone Forest consists of stone tablets that carry 229 characters of "dragon" written in various styles that appeared in the history of Chinese language.

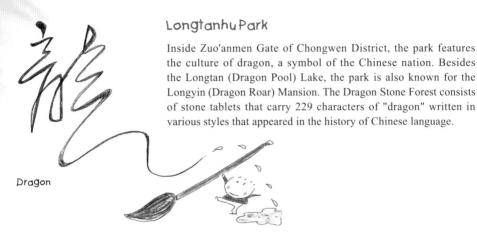

Dragon

Yuyuantan Park

Lying to the north of China Central Television on the eastern side of the 3rd Ring Road, the park is famous for the cherry blossoms that herald the arrival of spring. Every year, a cherry blossom festival is held in the park. There are some 2,000 Japanese flowering cherry trees in the park.

Zizhuyuan Park

Lying on the Baishiqiao Street, the park is known for bamboo. It is home to some 700,000 bamboos of more than 60 kinds. The most famous type is the purple bamboo *(zizhu)* after which the park is named.

Shidu

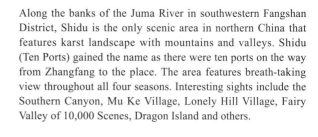

Along the banks of the Juma River in southwestern Fangshan District, Shidu is the only scenic area in northern China that features karst landscape with mountains and valleys. Shidu (Ten Ports) gained the name as there were ten ports on the way from Zhangfang to the place. The area features breath-taking view throughout all four seasons. Interesting sights include the Southern Canyon, Mu Ke Village, Lonely Hill Village, Fairy Valley of 10,000 Scenes, Dragon Island and others.

Wuling Mountain

The main peak of Yanshan Mountain Range stands at 2,118 m above sea level on the border of Beijing's Miyun District and Xinglong of Hebei Province. Mists and clouds shroud the mountain year-round. In the Qing Dynasty, it became part of the eastern imperial tombs. Today, the densely wooded mountain plays an important role in preserving and purifying water for the Miyun and Panjiakou reservoirs, two of the major sources for the water that Beijing residents drink everyday.

Kangxi Grassland

The summer resort lies to the west of Kangzhuang Village near the Badaling section of the Great Wall. The country's biggest horse racing ground can be found here.

Yunmeng Mountain

At the border of Miyun and Huairou districts, Yunmeng Mountain is praised as the smaller Huangshan Mountain, which is one of the country's most famous mountains in Anhui Province. The main peak of the mountain is 1,414 m high. The dense wood offers ideal routes for tracking.

Banbidian Forest Park

At 10 km to the south of Huangcun, Daxing District, the park is known for the pastoral scene. A special memorial wood here is open to the public. Newly weds can plant a tree together to mark their love. There are many types of trees to choose from for different occasions.

Taoranting Park

The park named after Taoran (Happy and Carefree) Pavilion is built to the northwest of Taoran Bridge on the southern 2nd Ring Road. The pavilion was built by Jiang Zao, a high-ranking official during the rule of Emperor Kangxi, in 1695 of the Qing Dynasty. Earth dug out of the two lakes near the pavilion has become a small hill. The Cibei Nunnery inside the park can be dated back to the Yuan Dynasty.

相当的

陶然

Very happy, carefree...

Qinglong Gorge

The Qinglong (Blue Dragon) Gorge in Huairou District offers a series of exciting activities centered on the Qinglong Dam. In bungee-jumping, the height can be 68 m. Downhill and rock climbing are also thrilling games at the valley.

Beijing Wildlife Park

At the safari in Yufa Town of Daxing District, visitors can find wolves, wild boars, lions and baboons living together. It is possible to see predators catching their prey. In another area, visitors are allowed to play with deer, roe, muntjac, squirrel and others.

Longqing Gorge

Lying in northern Yanqing District, Longqing Gorge is praised as the "Lijiang River (a famous picturesque river in Guilin of Guangxi) outside the Great Wall". Even in hottest summer, the area's temperature is about 5 C lower than that of downtown Beijing. As the ice won't melt until spring, the locals are fond of making ice sculptures. An ice lantern festival is held here every January and February.

Yunxiu Valley

Lying in northeastern Miyun District, the Yunxiu Valley has charming waters, red rocks and giant boulders left by glacial movement. The Miyun International Hunting Park is the biggest and best-equipped of its kind in northern China. There is also a frisbee shooting ground, where one can fully enjoy shooting.

Beijing World Park

The park that takes up 46.7 hectares lies in southwestern Fengtai District. The architectures are laid out according to the five continents and the water system resembles the four oceans of the world. Visitors can find the Japanese garden, Sydney's opera house, African aboriginal village, the White House and Golden Gate Bridge of the United States, windmills of Holland and other scenes along the way. It is an interesting place to catch glimpses of the diversified cultures of the world.

World Tour in Cartoons

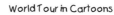

World Number Ones in Beijing

Beihai Park:
oldest existing imperial garden

Forbidden City:
biggest imperial palatial complex

Tian'anmen Square:
biggest square in urban center

Great Wall:
longest military defense work

Yunju Temple:
oldest and biggest library of Buddhist and Taoist classics carved on stone

Summer Palace:
most intact imperial garden

Peking Man Site at Zhoukoudian:
richest findings in paleoanthropology

Ming Tombs:
imperial cemetery with the biggest number of emperors

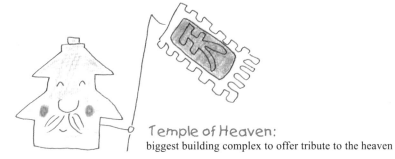

Temple of Heaven:
biggest building complex to offer tribute to the heaven

227000
Words

Yongle Bell:
a bell engraved with the biggest number of words in
the world — some 227,000 words of Buddhist and
Taoist scripture

Eight Sights of Yanjing (old Beijing)

Foggy Wood at Jimen (Jimen Yanshu)

At about 4 km to the northwest of Deshengmen Gate, there were the ruins of ancient Jizhou that could be dated back to the Liao and Yuan dynasties. It is said that the area was densely wooded. Even on sunny days, the moisture rising out of the leaves would make it appear to be foggy.

Sunset at the Golden Platform (Jintai Xizhao)

Jintai (Golden Platform) was located at Guandongdian of today's Jintai Street. There was a military training ground in the Qing Dynasty (1616-1911). The high platform in the center was called Jintai. Upon sunset, the last rays of sunlight would cast a golden spell over the platform for a while.

Moon over Lugou Bridge at Daybreak (Lugou Xiaoyue)

At dawn, when a crescent moon hangs low over the Lugou Bridge, one might see the Western Mountain and the ancient Sanggan River shrouded in mist. It would be an ideal traditional Chinese painting.

Bouncing Jade Spring (Yuquan Baotu)

The spring on Yuquan (Jade Spring) Hill of Beijing's western suburbs was called Number One Spring in the World. In the rule of Emperor Qianlong in the 18th century, the spring's water began reducing. But it is still one of the best springs in the city.

Layers of Green over Juyong Gate (Juyong Diecui)

One of the towers with the Juyong Gate of the Great Wall was built in a 15-km-long valley. The picturesque mountains covered in forests gained praise as "*Juyong Diecui*" (Layers of Green over Juyong Gate) as early as the Jin Dynasty (1115-1234). It was listed as the most famous scene of all eight sights in old Beijing.

Spring Shade at the Qiongdao Island (Qiongdao Chunyin)

This refers to the wooded area to the east of Qionghua Island in Beihai (North Sea) Park. With few architectures, the ancient trees arch over the quiet lake, making it a serene site in the busy capital.

Sunny Day after Snow at the West Mountain (Xishan Qingxue)

From the ruined Xiangshan Temple at the Fragrant Hill, one can climb up and reach Wenfeng (Hearing Wind) Pavilion and Chaoyang (Facing the Sun) Cave. At the waist of the mountain is a tablet written with the words "*Xishan Qingxue*" (Sunny Day after Snow at the West Mountain). Every winter, if one reaches the tablet after a snow, the visitor will be rewarded with a breath-taking bird's-eye view of the silvery mountains.

Autumn Breeze over the Ethereal Lake (Taiye Qiufeng)

The tablet bearing the four characters can be found in Shuiyunxie (Water & Cloud) Pavilion in Nanhai (South Sea) of downtown Beijing. The stone bridge between Zhonghai (Middle Sea) and Nanhai is called Jin'aoyudong (Golden Turtle and Jade Rainbow). The pavilion by its side is Shuiyunxie. As the clouds are reflected on the lake surface, the delicate pavilion seems to be a blossoming lotus flower.

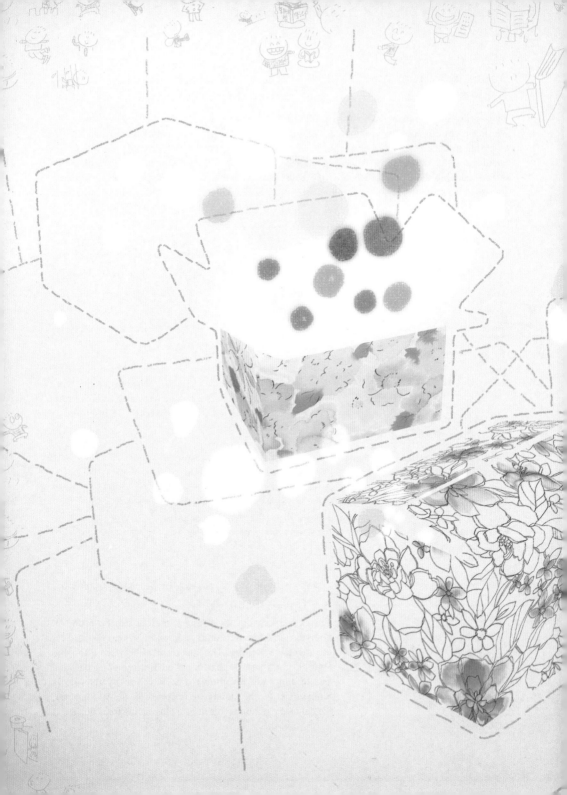

Bustling city life

Heaven of shopping

Wangfujing

Nicknamed "Golden Street", the world-famous pedestrian street is imbued with a deep cultural background. The biggest commercial center in Beijing enchants visitors with many century-old local shops such as China Photo Studio, Quanjude Restaurant, Shengxifu and others.

Cashier

Neiliansheng
Majuyuan
Tongshengtang
Zhangyiyuan
Shengxifu
Ruifuxiang
Tongshenghe
Tianhecheng
Heniantang

Qianmen-Dashilan

Newly furbished and reopened to the public, the area used to be the commercial center of old Beijing. Today, visitors can find the highest concentration of old brand names with a guarantee of quality service at the street that begins in the east from Qianmen Street and ends at Meishi Street in the west.

Xidan

Sitting at the geometric center of Beijing, the 6-km-long street is one of the capital's most developed areas of business and services. Xidan North Street is more developed than the southern part, with Xidan Shopping Mall, Zhong You Mall and other famous shopping centers standing side by side. Xidan Cultural Square is the largest recreational and shopping center in downtown Beijing.

Dongdan

The street from Dongdan to Dongsi is nicknamed "Silver Street" by white collars. The brightly decorated façades cater to different needs and reflect latest trends in the bustling cosmopolis.

Silk Street

Lying to the north of Jianguomenwai Street, the Silk Street has been moved into a building where one can find many souvenirs with strong Chinese characteristics. While its closeness to the embassy area brought the first visitors, the quality of commodities and the business acumen of the dealers have maintained growing attention of international visitors including tourists and dealers. Some foreigners have called the place "OK Street", "Small Hong Kong" or "Petit Paris".

Liulichang

Located outside Heping Gate, the street originated from the Qing Dynasty, when scholars from across the country lodged here to attend the imperial examination to choose civil officials. There are many shops for books, antiques and four treasures of the study — writing brush, ink stick, ink slab and *xuan* paper.

Four treasures of the study

Lufthansa Women's Street

At Dongsanhuan North Street, the market caters to women customers who can find scarves, jewelry, underwear, bags, shoes and anything that might attract a woman.

Panjiayuan Antiques Market

The market at Panjiayuan of Chaoyang District accommodates 3,000 stall owners from across the country, dealing in antiques like jadeware, arts and crafts, books, paintings and furniture. It is a "holy land" for antiques lovers hailing from across the world.

Beijing specialties

Babao Ink Paste

The red ink paste is used for seal. Made with some 30 procedures, the Babao (Eight Treasures) Ink Paste has a bright and pure color that guarantees clear and long-lasting prints.

Wang Mazi Scissors

Originated during the rule (1644-1661) of Emperor Shunzhi of the Qing Dynasty, the scissors were made at a store at Caishikou outside the Xuanwu Gate. It is said that the store's founder was a native of Shanxi Province and surnamed Wang. As Wang had pockmarks (*mazi* in Chinese) on his face, people called his store Wang Mazi Knife and Scissors Store. During Emperor Jiaqing's rule (1796-1820), Wang's grandson hang up a banner saying "Third Generation Wang Mazi". All the scissors made there have since carried the mark of Wang Mazi. As the Wang Mazi Scissors are sharp and black in color, people also call them "black tigers".

Chrysanthemum Liquor

This liquor is made on an esoteric recipe from the imperial distillery of the Qing Dynasty. Ginseng, agalloch eaglewood and some 20 kinds of precious medicinal herbs are used in making the transparent liquor that has a special fragrance and tastes sweet and mellow.

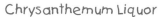

Wine

Osmanthus-Flower Wine

With a history of more than 3,000 years, the special product of Beijing is fermented with osmanthus flowers on the base of white wine. It is a high-quality nourishment.

Jinhu fiddle

With a high pitch and rich tones, the *jinhu* fiddle is the primary accompaniment of Peking Opera. There are strict requirements on its materials and production.

Peking Dough Figurine

Dough figurine is a folk art of high aesthetic value. With flour and glutinous rice powder as the chief materials, the colorful dough is made with pigment, paraffin wax, honey and other ingredients. The folk artist displays a dazzling skill in molding the shapeless dough into figurines. With a small knife made of bamboo, the artist carves out the figurines' facial features and applies dresses and ornaments swiftly. Elegant ladies, naughty children and legendary immortals are born within a minute.

Cloisonné

The art work originated in the years with the reign title of Jingtai (1450-1456) of Emperor Daizong of Ming Dynasty. As blue glaze is used extensively above the copper base, it gained the Chinese name Jingtailan. The making of a cloisonné work involves complicated procedures from tempering the copper base to sketching patterns with metal wire, applying blue glaze, firing it, polishing and gilding.

candied fruits

Candied fruits of Beijing

Candied fruits of Beijing are made with special procedures once used only in the imperial court. Made from fresh fruits such as apricot, pear and begonia, they taste sweet sour, with a mellowness of fruits.

Kite

The making and flying of kites in Beijing can be dated back to more than 300 years ago. In the past, people would carry enormous kites to join competitions outside the city. Traditional kites often feature intricate designs like butterfly, swift, dragonfly and masks of Peking Opera.

Old brand names in Beijing

Wear a hat from Majuyuan

Banknotes from the Four Heng's tucked in the waist

Don clothes from the Eight Xiang's

Walk in shoes from Neiliansheng

Majuyuan, Neiliansheng, Eight Xiang's and Four Heng's

In the past, some Beijing people showcased their high social status with commodities from famous brand name stores, most of which were located around Qianmen area. Majuyuan was famous for making hats and it was founded in 1817. Neiliansheng, founded in 1853, was renown for high quality shoes. The Eight Xiang's refer to stores selling cloth and silk and they all had the word "*xiang*" (auspiciousness) in their names: Ruilinxiang, Qianxiangyi, Ruishengxiang, Ruifuxiang, Yihexiang, Ruizengxiang, Ruichengxiang and Guangshengxiang. Sadly, Ruifuxiang is the only one still in business. The Four Heng's refer to old banking houses whose names all began with "*heng*" (everlasting): Hengli, Henghe, Hengxing and Hengyuan. A typical well-off old Beijing resident would be proud to wear a hat from Majuyuan, don clothes from the Eight Xiang's, walk in shoes from Neiliansheng, with banknotes from the Four Heng's tucked in his waist.

Tongrentang

Perhaps the most famous name for traditional Chinese medicine, Tongrentang was founded in 1669 and made pills, powder, ointment and pellet of its own prescriptions. Since it was founded, the generations of owners always adhered to the motto of "never omitting even one of the complicated procedures, never reducing any bit of the expensive materials". In 1723 of Emperor Yongzheng's rule, Tongrentang began supplying medicine for the imperial court. It served eight emperors in a period of 188 years. Today, the many branches of Tongrentang still attract customers with self-made medicines of high quality.

Donglaishun

In the past, many Muslim restaurants serving mutton hotpots had the word *"shun"* (smooth) in their names: Donglaishun, Xilaishun, Nanlaishun and Youyishun. In the early 1910s, Donglaishun had established its fame with tender meat and carefully prepared seasoning.

Shun;smooth

砂锅居
Shaguoju

Eight Ju's

"Ju" is a traditional word for restaurant. There were eight famous restaurants in Beijing that all had the word *"ju"* in their names: Shaguoju, Tianxingju, Tianranju, Dingheju, Guangheju, Tongheju, Yishengju and Huixianju. The most famous one was Shaguoju, which opened in 1741 at Gangwashi of Xisi South Street. Its name comes from a huge pottery pot that measured 1 m deep and 1.3 m in diameter. The restaurant used the pot to prepare delicious meat of the northern Chinese flavor.

Paraphernalia of the study (Rongbaozhai, Daiyuexuan, Boguzhai, Wenkuitang)

Rongbaozhai is located on the Liulichang West Street and deals with books and paintings. It has a history of over 300 years. Daiyuexuan lies on the Liulichang East Street, focusing on writing brush of Huzhou, Zhejiang Province and inkslab of Huizhou, Anhui Province. Boguzhai was founded in 1850 by Zhu Jinfan and deals with paper for calligraphy and painting. Wenkuitang's history can be dated back to 1881. It collects, prints and sells ancient classics, especially their original and precious copies.

Quanjude Roast Duck

Founded in 1864, Quanjude deviated from the traditional way of preparing roast duck. The chefs will send the duck to the customer with a small cart and display the dazzling techniques in slicing the meat. Each duck must produce at least 120 slices, each piece carrying both skin and meat with fat and lean parts.

Wangzhihe
Fermented
Bean
Curd

Wangzhihe Fermented Bean Curd

Created in the rule (1662-1722) of Emperor Kangxi of the Qing Dynasty, Wangzhihe fermented bean curd has a strong smelling that is repulsive for many but whose unique taste attracts more lovers.

Bianyifang

Founded in 1416 of the Ming Dynasty, Bianyifang champions a roast duck prepared differently from those of Quanjude. Instead of simply hanging the duck inside a huge furnace, Bianyifang chefs inject special soup into the duck and the furnace doesn't have flames. The roast duck of Bianyifang has crispy skin and tender meat inside.

Bianyifang

I accept no present this Spring Festival, except for ...

Douyichu

Opened in 1738, the restaurant serves *shaomai* — steamed dumpling with the dough frilled at the top. Emperor Qianlong once tasted the dumpling here and granted the restaurant a calligraphy work of three words *"dou yi chu"*, meaning finding all the delicacies at one place. The restaurant still enjoys a thriving business as its dumplings have maintained the good quality.

Kaorouji and Kaorouwan

Kaorouji is a 100-year-old restaurant near the Yindian Bridge of Shichahai. Kaorouwan is another restaurant in Xuanwumen Inner Street. Together they were called "Wan in the south and Ji in the north". Kaorouji is known for carefully chosen lamb prepared with meticulous care. Kaorouwan was founded by a Muslim surnamed Wan. The beef served here is prepared in complicated procedures to meet the pickiest connoisseurs.

Eight Mansions

Around the 1900s, there were eight famous restaurants whose names ended with *"lou"* (mansion): Zhengyanglou, Taifenglou, Xinfenglou, Wandelou, Yuebinlou, Qingyunlou, Dongxinglou and Huiyuanlou. Most of the eight restaurants were founded by people from Shandong Province, whose cuisine — named *Lucai* — is seen as one of the major genres of cuisine in the country. Zhengyanglou, opened in 1843, is the most famous and provides big crabs from Bohai Sea in autumn accompanied with liquor from eastern Beijing.

Art zones

Shangyuan Art Village

The Taohuayu scenic area in Xingshou Town of Changping District has attracted painters, poets, art critics, collectors and art professors. They purchased the rights to use the land and designed their own houses as part of their art works.

Artist

Critic

Songzhuang Art Village

At about 6 km to the east of Tongzhou District, Songzhuang Village has become a SOHO area with some 400 Chinese artists from outside Beijing.

Yellow River Symphony Made in Songzhuang

In the 1950s, New York artists moved into dilapidated industrial buildings to live and create. The spacious factories with low rent have become fashionable among artists. There are also similar centers of art in Beijing.

Songzhuang

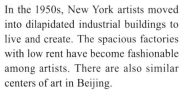

Feijia village

Huajiadi Art Zone

Located inside Wangjing residential compound, the art zone is home to many famous artists.

Huajiadi

Feijia Village

The village is located at the Laiguangying East Street to the north of the 5th Ring Road and near the Airport Expressway. It is close to Wangjing, China Central Academy of Fine Arts and 798 Factory.

East End Art

East End Art

The newly developed modern art zone is close to the Airport Expressway and can be reached by Bus No 402. It is just 1 km away from 798 Factory. Artists, galleries, institutions, design studios and media offices have been set up at the area with a strong futurist feel.

Art

Huantie Art Zone

Huantie

E. 5th Ring

Dashanzi Roundabout

Wuyuanqiao Jingshun st Exit

Jingshun St.

798

Jiuxianqiao St.

Huantie Art Zone

At the northeastern part of Beijing is a huge circle of rails that was constructed for testing new trains. There are about seven art zones scattered here like tribes, involving at least 100 art studios.

Beijing No.1 Art Base

The art zone covers nearly 2 sq km at Hegezhuang Village of Cuigezhuang Township, Chaoyang District. Some 30 art institutions and nearly 100 artists and collectors have come to the place with six function areas like international arts trade and traditional Chinese arts.

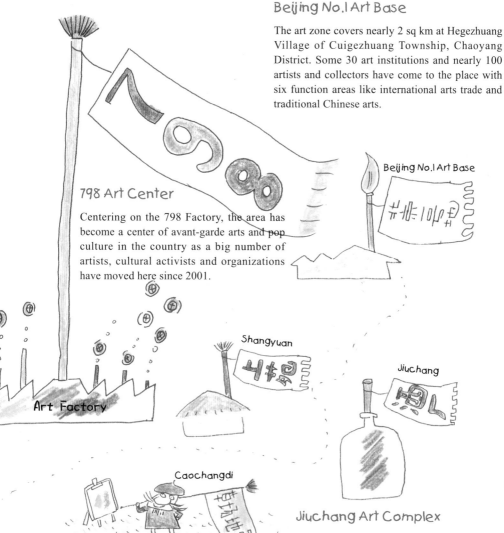

798 Art Center

Centering on the 798 Factory, the area has become a center of avant-garde arts and pop culture in the country as a big number of artists, cultural activists and organizations have moved here since 2001.

Beijing No.1 Art Base

Art Factory

Shangyuan

Jiuchang

Caochangdi

Jiuchang Art Complex

Located at Beihuqu of Beiyuan in Chaoyang District, Jiuchang Art Complex is reconstructed on the base of Chaoyang District Erguotou Liquor Factory that has a history of 30 years. More than 100 Chinese and overseas art dealers and artists have gathered here, which has become an ideal site of artistic creations.

Caochangdi Art Zone

At about 3 km away from 798 Factory, Caochangdi has attracted many major domestic art institutions and artists. Galleries like Sanshang Art, Tzuchinhsuan, Platform China, Art Corridor and Ai Weiwei Art Studio are located here.

Beijing for gourmets

东华门小吃街 西食街 隆福寺 鱼街 天安门食 阜食街 阳首街 五道村食街

卤煮火烧 炸灌肠 爆肚 炒肝 锅贴 豆汁 门钉肉饼 驴打滚 褡裢火烧 天福号酱肘子

Snack streets

Xisi Food Street

From the crossroad of Xinjiekou in the north to Xisi in the south, the short street takes less than 20 minutes to walk through. But there are many famous restaurants that have established fame in the past century or even longer: Xinchuan Noodles Restaurant, Qingfeng *Jiaozi* Dumpling Restaurant, Old Xi'an Restaurant, Yanji Restaurant, Shaguoju Restaurant and so on.

Longfusi Snacks Street

The narrow street becomes bustling with life on summer nights. Tourists can savor whatever food that catches their fancy from stalls that line up for 100 meters. Each stand's owner has invented a special way to call customers' attention.

Donghuamen Snacks Street

The well-known snacks street is located at the entrance of the Wangfujing Street. It is the only open-air snacks street in Beijing. Delicacies from across the country are sold at more than 100 stalls.

Guijie Street

Nicknamed Ghost Street, it begins from the western end of Dongzhimen Overpass on the Eastern 2nd Ring Road to the eastern end of Jiaodaokou East Street. The street runs through the embassy area, which gifts it with a special advantage. A total of 148 eateries line the street of 1,000 m. There is no other place in Beijing where restaurants are run at such a high concentration.

Guang'anmen Food Street

Lying in southern Beijing from Liuliqiao to Hufangqiao, this street features hot and spicy dishes such as Malayouhuo, Lilaodie (specializing in crabs) and Tanyutou (fish) that hail from Sichuan Province. The Muslim restaurants near Niujie are also very popular.

Fangzhuang Food Street

Fangzhuang is one of the capital's largest residential areas that appeared in the 1990s. There are more than 30 major restaurants along the "food street" that attract old and new customers every night. From east to west, some of the famous eateries include Shunfeng Seafood Mansion, Daqinghua *Jiaozi* Restaurant, Daziran Northeast Mansion, Luoluo Sour Fish Soup, Lotus Seed Porridge, Douyichu, Shunyifu, Jinshancheng Chongqing Cuisine, Jinhanxin, Tongliyuan Mansion and Jindingxuan.

Xiaoyunlu Food Street

Xiaoyunlu lies between Sanyuandong Bridge on the 3rd Ring Road and Xiaoyun Bridge on the 4th Ring Road. One can find famous restaurants like Xiyan, Eryue'er, Jinshancheng, Jinsanyuan and Bellagio Café.

Asian Games Village Food Street

Most of the restaurants in the Asian Games Village can be found along Huizhong North Street, Datun Street and Anhuili Community. Some of the restaurants are Xibei Youmian Village, Tanggong Seafood, Huangjihuang, Fulou and others.

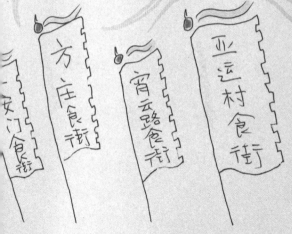

Beijing traditional snacks

Shuanyangrou (dip-boiled mutton slices)

The dish became popular after Manchurian rulers conquered Beijing to establish the Qing Dynasty in 1644. The best mutton slices come from wether that weighs 20 to 25 kg each and is bred in Uzhumqin Banner of western Inner Mongolia Autonomous Region. Dip-boiled in a copper pot, the slices taste well with different styles of seasoning.

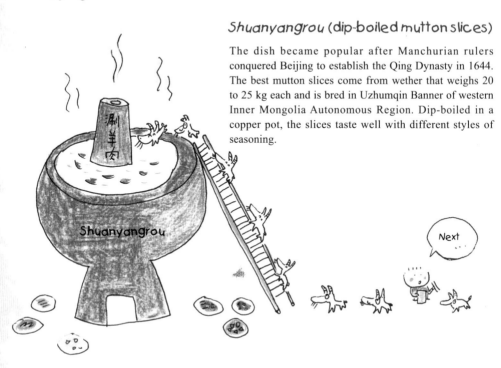

Shuanyangrou

Next

Manhan quanxi (complete Manchurian and Han banquet)

Originated from the rule (1662-1722) of Emperor Kangxi, which was the peak of the Qing Dynasty, the banquet was of the highest level that the Emperor gave to foreign dignitaries and high-ranking officials. Deemed as the most famous banquet in the history of Chinese cuisine, the banquet includes 108 dishes and 44 snacks of both Manchurian and Han Chinese origin. It would take a connoisseur three days to savor all the courses.

Your Majesty, shall we begin...

Tan Family Dishes

Originated from the rule (1862-1874) of Emperor Tongzhi, the dishes were designed for governmental officials. Among the hundreds of dishes, swallow nest and shark fin are the most famous. The courses include both southern dishes that are tender, crispy and fresh, and northern tastes that are mellow and soft.

Yushan (imperial cuisine)

Also named *Fangshan*, the dishes were served for the imperial family. Each formal meal consists of 128 courses whose materials come from the mountains and the seas. Extreme care is given to the color, fragrance, taste and shape of every dish that represents the cream of Chinese cuisine.

卤煮火烧　白　炒肝
炸灌肠　　火暴肚
　　　锅贴　豆汁
门钉肉饼　驴打滚
褡裢火烧　　焦圈
天福号酱肘子

Beijing Snacks
京味小吃

Luzhu huoshao (pot-stewed pancake)

Pieces of pancake, pig lung, pig intestines and bean curd are stewed with soy sauce in a big pot. The rich taste is perfectly matched with the varied texture.

Zhaguanchang (sausage)

Starch and red koji rice are mixed to make something like sausage. It is sliced and fried before seasoned with garlic juice and salty water.

Guotie (lightly fried dumpling)

Shaped like *jiaozi* dumpling but smaller, *guotie* is lightly fried with a crispy surface and contains varied fillings.

Dalian huoshao (pancake)

The pancake is golden in color and delicious in taste.

Douzhi

The fermented drink is made from the water used in grinding green beans. Beijing people love this drink with a unique taste.

Chaogan (fried liver)

A famous snack in Beijing, it goes well with small steamed stuffed bun.

Baodu (quick-boiled tripe)

Fresh tripe of cow or sheep is thoroughly cleaned and cut into strips. A few minutes into the boiling water, the strips are taken out and dipped in sesame paste, chopped Chinese onion and other seasoning. It tastes crispy, fragrant and tender.

Tianfuhao jiangzhouzi

The pork joint simmered in marinated sauce made by the old restaurant Tianfuhao used to be favored by the imperial court. The upper part of a leg of pork has fat that is not greasy, lean meat that is not dry and a skin that is tenacious. The delicacy tastes mellow and fragrant.

Mending roubing (meat-stuffed pancake)

Mending means the protruding fist-sized nails on the gates of palaces. The meat-stuffed pancake gets this name because of its close resemblance to the nails.

Jiaoquan (deeply fried doughnut)

The double doughnut is deeply fried until it is brown and crispy.

Flavors from across the country

Shanghai cuisine

Simple and reasonably priced, Shanghai cuisine excels in dishes braised in brown sauce, or stir-fried before stewing. The presence of sugar adds much color and mellow taste to the dishes that can be found in most households in Shanghai.

Huaiyang cuisine

The dishes from the middle and lower reaches of the Yangtze and Huaihe rivers are prepared with great techniques on the knife and fire. Stew, braise, simmer, steam, fry and stir-fry are some of the commonly employed cooking methods. Most dishes of Huaiyang cuisine are based on water products that are freshly caught. Yangzhou of Jiangsu Province is the center of Huaiyang cuisine. A typical dish is the large crab meatball simmered in soup.

Guangdong cuisine

Also called *Yuecai*, the cuisine makes good use of materials from a dazzling array of sources. Great care is given to precision in matching the materials and seasoning. Many dishes serve as good decorations. Though the taste is not pungent, a careful gourmet can discern constant improvements in even the simplest homely dishes.

Hunan cuisine

Known as *Xiangcai,* the dishes come from the mountains of western Hunan Province, the drainage area of Xiangjiang River and the Dongting Lake. Prepared with much oil and rendered in deep color, the dishes are tender and fragrant, sour and hot.

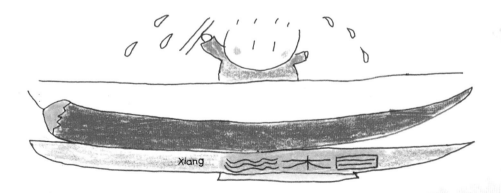

Sichuan cuisine

Simply known as *Chuancai*, it is one of four major Chinese cuisines along with *Lucai* (from Shandong), Yuecai (from Guangdong) and *Huaiyangcai* (from the middle and lower reaches of the Yangtze and Huaihe rivers). With a long history, Sichuan cuisines are known for the generous use of hot pepper and Chinese prickly ash.

Chuan
(short for Sichuan)

Shandong cuisine

Also called *Lucai*, the dishes come from East China's Shandong Province. The meticulously prepared dishes are slightly salty but maintain the freshness and tender texture of the raw materials.

Vegetarian dishes

There are vegetarian dishes for the laymen and monks of Buddhism and Taoism. They invariably employ the rich variety of fungus and bean curd to imitate the appearance and texture of meat. Upon the first bite, one might be surprised at the great energy invested for imitating pork, fish and chicken.

Foreign flavors

Japanese ryoli

Japanese food always delights the eater with apt use of the season's best produce. The Japanese take great pride in the special products of each region, which gives rise to diversified dishes of great aesthetic value.

German cuisine

German dishes always appear simple as the vegetables and meats are prepared in traditional methods.

French cuisine

French cuisine gives painstaking attention to the freshness of raw materials in each season. They attain perfection in all the senses. Representing a graceful, romantic air, a genuine French meal could cost some 7,000 yuan for each customer.

Minority flavors

Muslim restaurants

Beef, mutton, chicken and duck are the main sources of meat for Muslim restaurants. The dishes are fried, stir-fried or dip-boiled. Plant oil, salt, vinegar and sugar are commonly used.

Xinjiang cuisine

Noodles, *nang* pancake, beef and mutton are what satisfy the many minorities in Northwest China's Xinjiang Uygur Autonomous Region. Onion, tomato and hot pepper are added with *ziran* (a special local seasoning), pepper powder and vinegar to make the dishes sour, spicy and tasty.

Tibetan cuisine

With buttered tea and *qingke* (highland barley) wine, one may find it hard not to fall in love with Tibetan food, such as *zamba*, a staple made of fried *qingke* flour with butter and seasoning. Beef and mutton are dried or simply boiled to furnish a big banquet.

Dai cuisine

Dai minority lives mainly in Southwest China's Yunnan Province. The dishes are sour, sweet, bitter and hot, with sour as the reigning taste. The cooking techniques of the Dai people cover a wide range from baking to frying, boiling, steaming and preserving. Many insects and wild herbs are also included in the dishes for daring customers.

Bars

Houhai

Along the banks of the Shichahai Lake, more than 100 bars have appeared among the willows, drawing customers' attention with unique decorations.

Sanlitun

On the southern part of Sanlitun Street in Chaoyang District, Sanlitun has become a famous area for more than 100 bars featuring various styles since the first bar opened here in 1996.

Beijing folk
culture

Festivals and folk customs

Spring Festival

Spring Festival is the most important traditional festival for Chinese people. For the past 500 years, Beijing has been the country's political and cultural center, which brings colorful customs to the Spring Festival in Beijing. An old lullaby sums up all the activities leading up to the Spring Festival that falls in January or February: "Old lady, there's no hurry — the Spring Festival is near after *laba* (the 8th day of the 12th lunar month); after eating the *laba* porridge, the 23rd day will soon arrive; offer pumpkin-shaped candy to the God of Stove on the 23rd day; clean the house on the 24th; make bean curd on the 25th; buy meat on the 26th; kill a cock on the 27th; prepare the flour on the 28th; make steamed bun on the 29th; stay awake on the night of the 30th and go to visit relatives and friends on the first day of the New Year".

Lantern Festival

One of the main traditional festivals in China, it falls on the 15th day of the first lunar month. In the Ming and Qing dynasties, emperors would go to the Temple of Heaven on this day to hold grand ceremonies praying for good harvest. Every Chinese family would try to stay together on this night and enjoy *yuanxiao* (sweet dumplings made of glutinous rice flour) while watching the full moon. People would throng to Dengshi or Changdian to watch the colorful lanterns. Before the 1900s, governmental agencies would resume working between the 19th to the 21st days of the first lunar month after the Spring Festival celebrations. Farmers would also begin tilling the fields and sowing seeds.

Temple fairs

Temple fairs are like carnivals for local people. They originated from the Liao Dynasty more than 1,000 years ago and most are held around the Spring Festival. Various folk arts and performances are staged, many snacks and toys entice visitors. There used to be eight major sites for the temple fairs in Beijing.

Temple of Earth:
The oldest Spring Festival temple fair in Beijing, a typical example of temple fair held in the garden.

Longtan Lake:
Many traditional cultural and athletic activities are held here.

Dongyue Temple:
The temple fair started more than 300 years ago at this temple worshiping the God of Mt Taishan, with the theme of "fu" (happiness).

Baiyunguan Taoist Temple:
The temple fair here has a boisterous air with traditional performances like lion dance, stilt-walking, land-boat and others.

Changdian:
Originated from the rule (1522-1566) of Emperor Jiajing of the Ming Dynasty, this is the biggest, most influential and famous event of all eight temple fairs.

Daguanyuan:
Held at the park built according to the classic novel *A Dream of the Red Chamber,* the temple fair includes folk crafts, skating, extreme sports, kungfu and drum dances among others.

Lianhuachi:
There are more than 100 activities in nine categories at the temple fair such as dance, folk opera, acrobatics, games, snacks and exhibitions.

Shijingshan Park:
The temple fair here features overseas flavors in songs and dances, as well as cuisines.

Daguanyuan Spring Gala

During the Spring Festival, a gala is held at Daguanyuan and many performances are staged there.

Daguanyuan

Duanwu Festival

In the Spring and Autumn Period, Qu Yuan (ca. 339-278 BC), a royal minister of the Dukedom of Chu, was wronged by the Duke and despaired that the enemy would soon conquer his homeland. The great statesman who excelled in poetry held a stone and threw himself into the Miluo River of today's Hunan Province. To commemorate the patriotic noble man, the people threw *zongzi* (pyramid-shaped dumpling made of glutinous rice and wrapped in bamboo leaves or reeds) into the river and raced dragon-shaped boats to salvage him. The tradition gradually became the Duanwu Festival that falls on the 5th day of the 5th lunar month.

Mid-Autumn Festival

The 15th day of the 8th lunar month lies in the middle of the three autumn months, thus the festival is named "*zhongqiu*" — mid-autumn. As the bright, full moon shines in the sky, every Chinese family would sit together and enjoy moon cake, watermelon, crabs and other delicacies, while talking about ancient tales related with the moon.

Yanqing Snow & Ice Festival

Between Jan 15 to Feb 28, an exhibition of ice sculptures and lanterns is held at Longqing Gorge of Yanqing County.

Where the peach blossoms are...

Peach Blossom Festival

Every April, the Beijing Botanical Garden hosts a month-long festival for visitors to admire the peach blossoms.

Cherry Blossom Festival

Also held in April, the festival takes place at Yuyuantan Park where one can also take a boat ride to better admire the cherry blossoms.

Marriage customs

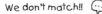

Matching the birthdays

Old Beijing residents paid great attention to the matching of the hour, date, month and year of the young man and woman. Special geomancers were invited to see if the two would match or one might bring harm to the other in married life.

Meeting the prospective family

When the birthdays of the two young people were proven to be a good match, their parents would meet on an auspicious day with the matchmaker in either family.

Greeting the bride

Upon the auspicious day, the bridegroom would lead the team to greet the bride at her home. But the gate of the bride's family would be shut tightly and the bridegroom or a member of the team would ask persistently and hand in a red envelope containing money before the door was opened. The team would then splash copper coins in the courtyard. After many complicated procedures, the bride finally set foot in the sedan chair prepared by her betrothed and headed for her new home.

Wedding ceremony Double Happiness

When the team brought the bride in her sedan chair back to the bridegroom's family, she also faced a shut gate, which was said to be a lesson to teach the woman to be humble and obedient. After much pounding on the door, the sedan chair was carried into the courtyard. But the bride would have to walk or be carried over a basin of fire as another way of gaining blessings. The relatives of the bride were then invited to the banquet.

Paying tribute to ancestors

After the bride and bridegroom did obeisance to Heaven and Earth, their parents and each other, they must pay homage to the ancestors. To become a formal member of the family, the bride also needed approval of her husband's ancestors.

boisterous banquet

Initial engagement

When both families found the proposed marriage acceptable, the young man's family would send the young woman's family small gifts as the initial engagement. There were no fixed rules in the gifts. Most families would put golden bracelets, rings, *ruyi* (a wand shaped like "s" to mean fulfilling one's wishes) and other small jewelry into two boxes. Another two boxes would contain fine cloth and outfits.

Choosing the wedding day

The engagement day was seldom set in the last lunar month and the wedding day was rarely fixed in the first lunar month. And the number "8" is seen as the best date.

Etiquettes

Formal engagement

Once the wedding date was settled, the formal engagement would be carried out in a grand ceremony. The so-called "dragon-phoenix folded cards", which served like marriage certificates, were exchanged between the two families. In addition, four boxes of more valuable betrothal gifts were sent to the bride's home. After this ceremony, either side normally would not break the vow.

Sending the dowry

The bride's family would send the dowry to her future husband's home one or two days before the wedding.

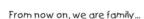

Dowry

From now on, we are family...

bride's home

The bride returns home

On the third or the fourth day after the wedding, the bride was allowed to return to her own family. Her husband accompanied her, but they had to go back to his home to spend the night.

Hutong lanes, siheyuan courtyards, old city walls

Labyrinth of *hutong* lanes

There was an old saying that goes: There are 3,600 *hutong* lanes with names, but the anonymous lanes are more than the hairs of a cow. By the end of the Ming Dynasty in the 17th century, Beijing had some 600 *hutong* lanes. The number increased to 978 in the Qing Dynasty and 1,330 in the mid-19th century. There are still 459 lanes with names in Beijing. Like Peking Opera and the Beijing dialect, *hutong* is full of Beijing flavor and the fountainhead of many folk tales and customs. According to the *Book of Rites* compiled in the Spring and Autumn Period more than 2,500 years ago, a city should be square in shape and had three gates on each side that measured 9 *li* (4.5 km). Inside, nine streets broad enough for nine chariots to ride alongside should be constructed from north to south and from east to west. The crisscrossing lanes of central Beijing have developed from Yuan Dynasty about 900 years ago. The Mongolian rulers of Yuan Dynasty designed residential areas and governmental offices into square zones. Rows of houses were built inside each zone, which was locked at night. When developing economy made it unnecessary to lock the zones any more, the walls were torn down and the narrow lanes among the rows of houses became *hutong*. To ensure longest possible sunshine and evade the chilling northern wind, most houses in *hutong* face the south and have side rooms on east and west sides of the main room. The making of the *hutong* lanes signified the real formation of Beijing.

Name of hutong

Dao, lu, jie, xiang, hutong have been traditional terms for streets, paths, alleys and lanes. The names of Beijing's *hutong* are very interesting and come from different historical background. They reflect the city's long history and rich cultural heritage.

Named after celebrities:
Wenchengxiang Hutong,
Shijia Hutong, etc

Named after landmarks or historical ruins:
Xisi, Dongsi, etc

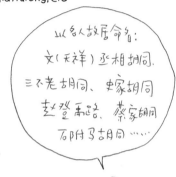

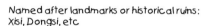

Named after scenic spots:
Tieshi Zi (Iron Lion) Hutong, etc

Named after businesses:
Luomashi (Horse and Mule Fair) ,etc

Named after landmarks or historical ruins

Gongyuan Toutiao (1st Lane) and Ertiao (2nd Lane) at Jianguomen Inner Street were named after Gongyuan, the site for scholars to take the imperial examination to choose civil officials in the Ming and Qing dynasties. Guozijian Road of Andingmen Inner Street is named after Guozijian, or Imperial College, which was the highest educational administration in Yuan, Ming and Qing dynasties. Dongdan and Xidan were named as they were located to the east or west of the ornamental archways that were built in odd number (*dan* in Chinese). As for Dongsi and Xisi, they gained the name because of four archways between them.

Named after celebrities

Such places abound in number. Wenchengxiang Hutong is named after Wen Tianxiang (1236-1283), a prime minister (*chengxiang*) who died defending the Song Dynasty. Sanbulao Hutong refers to Zheng He (1371-1433), who commanded the royal fleet to sail across Southeast Asia and reached Africa in seven expeditions. Zhaodengyu Street and Tonglinge Street commemorate Generals Zhao Dengyu (1898-1937) and Tong Linge (1892-1937) who died defending Beijing against Japanese assaults at the beginning of the War of Resistance Against Japanese Invasion (1937-1945).

Named after scenic spots

Beijing people are fond of beautiful scenery, which is reflected in the apt names such as Liuyin (Willow Shade) Street, Shibei (Stone Stele) Hutong, Jinyuchi (Gold Fish Pond), Jintaili (Inside the Golden Platform) and Baihua (Hundred Flowers) Hutong where many flowers were planted.

Named after businesses

Such places reflect the businesses that once thrived in the area. In Dongcheng District, there are the Guozi Alley for the fruit business and Dengshikou where lanterns were once sold and displayed in the Spring Festival. In Chongwen District, Huashi, Ciqikou and Xianyukou are named for flower, ceramics and fresh fish. In Xuanwu District, Caishikou, Niujie and Luomashi are so named because of the fairs on vegetable, beef, horse and mule.

Best-known hutong lanes in Beijing

Narrowest hutong:
   Xiaolaba Hutong (less than 0.6 m wide at the northern entrance)

Only remaining bridge spanning a hutong
   Guanyinyuan Bridge in Rufuli

One of the broadest existing hutong lanes:
   Lingjing Hutong (32.18 m at the broadest place)

One of the shortest existing hutong lanes:
   Yichidajie (only 25.23 m long, but it has become part of Yangmeizhu Xiejie)

One of the longest existing hutong lanes:
   Dongxijiaominxiang (3 km long)

Hutong with the biggest number of curves:
   Jiuwan Hutong

Oldest hutong:
   Zhuanta Hutong (which first appeared in the Six Dynasties period from AD 222 to 589)

Only existing glazed archway:
   Dongyue Temple Archway at the northern end of Shenlu Street

Only existing arched gate with brick carving:
   No 15 courtyard in Dongmianhua Hutong

Hutong with the most curves...

Oldest hutong...

Narrowest hutong...

Shortest hutong...

Broadest hutong...

Most...

Residential compound with multiple families

Commonly called *"da zayuanr"*, such compounds can be found in the northern and southern parts of old Beijing where the poor used to live. Such compounds could accommodate several or dozens of families and the living condition was far from ideal.

Siheyuan courtyards

Siheyuan is a unique residential compound in Beijing. The name means that the houses enclose upon the central courtyard. The main room must face south, and the kitchen and toilet should be located to the left and right sides of the main room. The rooms are given different importance according to their location and the residents living in them also differ in status. The main room is reserved for the senior-most man of the family and his wife. The northern rooms should be three or five in number and never be in even number. The eastern rooms are also important and appropriate as living rooms. But one dining room should be allocated among the eastern rooms.

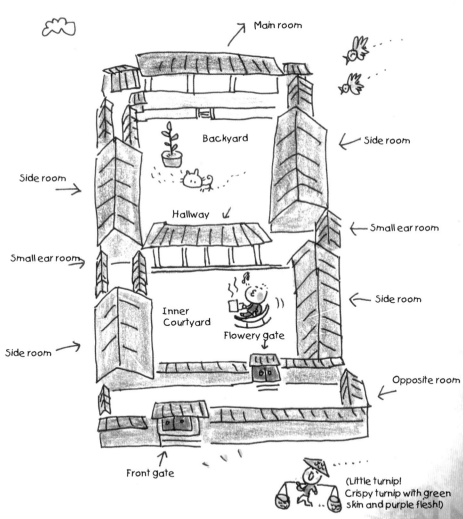

The city of Beijing

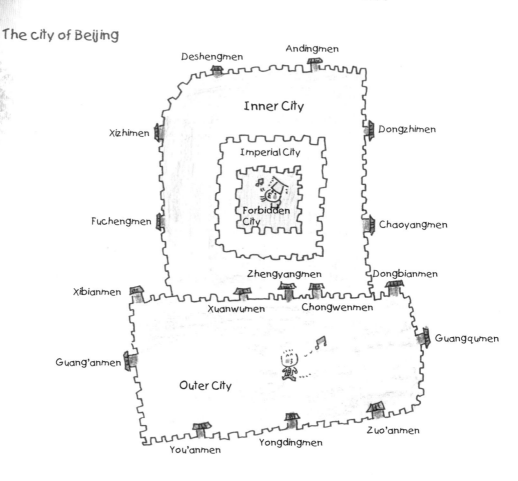

Though Beijing has been the nation's capital for many centuries, most of the remaining ancient architectures belong to the Ming and Qing dynasties. The city used to have the country's most complete defense system, composed with the palatial city, imperial city, inner city and outer city. The grand city walls encircling the city had gates, citadels, turrets, platforms and a city moat. The gates were designed according to the level of importance and location on the walls of palatial, imperial, inner and outer cities. There were four palatial gates, four imperial gates, nine inner gates and seven outer gates. The nine inner gates are: Desheng, Anding, Xizhi, Dongzhi, Fucheng, Chaoyang, Zhengyang, Xuanwu and Chongwen. In the 20th century, the palatial city has been preserved as the Palace Museum and its adjacent areas. The imperial city only has the Tian'anmen Rostrum. The wall of the inner city still has Zhengyang Gate, the turret and southeastern watchtower of Desheng Gate, and a passage of broken wall at Chongwen Gate. The walls of the outer city have been totally ruined, though the Yongding Gate has been rebuilt at its original site.

Peking Opera

Peking Opera is seen as the cream of Chinese culture. It gained the name as it was formed in Beijing (known as Peking) some 200 years ago on the basis of several more ancient folk operas. Peking Opera is a performance art that combines singing, dancing and martial arts. Even when the characters are simply speaking, the tone is very musical. There are four major roles: men, women, men with painted face and clowns. Each type is further differentiated according to the age, social status and whether they are good or evil.

Folk arts in performance

Beijing folk arts in performance are quite varied. Some of the more famous ones are *Jingyun Dagu*, *Meihua Dagu*, *Xihe Dagu*, *Danxian* and *Beijing Qinshu* which all have a rich repertoire of ancient tales with musical accompaniment.

Acrobatics

Zaji, or acrobatics, has developed from folk arts, magic shows and other cunning tricks popular among the common people. *Records of the Historian* says that the shows had appeared as early as the Shang Dynasty some 3,500 years ago. The elegance and awesome poses of Bijing acrobatics have won it a special place in the world arena.

Master Rabbit

The clay figurine is said to be modeled upon the legendary rabbit in the palace of the moon. Wearing a red robe over helmet, the statue holds a stick that is used to grind medicinal herbs. A light layer of rouge is applied to its face, which looks solemn but handsome. Upon the Mid-Autumn Festival, the families in Beijing would worship the rabbit, offering melons, vegetables, beans and others, to thank the deity for bringing good fortunes and happiness. The Master Rabbit is sometimes worshiped with a Lady Rabbit at its side.

Xiangsheng crosstalk

Xiangsheng is an art of humor that is unique in Beijing. Speech, imitation, poking fun and singing are the four main skills each actor or actress must master. A *xiangsheng* performance can involve one or two, or even more actors or actresses. Master Hou Baolin (1917-1993) once created the peak of traditional *xiangsheng*. Guo Degang, a young actor who strives to revitalize classic shows while creating modern pieces, has gained enormous popularity in recent years.

So bright a gleam on the foot of my bed. Could there have been a frost already? Lifting myself to look, I found that it was moonlight. Sinking back again, I am Guo Degang.

In the Quiet Night (Jing Ye Si) is a famous poem by Tang Dynasty poet Li Bai. Witter Bynner translated it as "So bright a gleam on the foot of my bed. Could there have been a frost already? Lifting myself to look, I found that it was moonlight. Sinking back again, I thought suddenly of home". But xiangsheng comedian Guo Degang changed the last line to 'I am Guo Degang', which rhymes with the poem perfectly though making no sense. Nevertheless, he won the audience's laughter and the new line became his pet phrase.

Clothing

When the Qing Dynasty settled its capital in Beijing nearly 400 years ago, the Manchurian rulers dictated that short coat, folded sleeve and plaited hair were the code of dress for men and banned the loose robes with broad sleeves and bound hair as worn by previous times.

During the Qing Dynasty, men had the front rim of their hair trimmed neatly and the hair was bound into a long plait, which gained the infamous name "pigtail". Every man wore a hat, which mainly included the official and the casual types. The round official hats were made of leather and satin. A red silk plait atop the hat carried a big jewel of red, blue or gold color according to the official ranking. A tube beneath the jewel contained a bunch of peacock tail feathers. The highest-level officials had three glowing barbules amid the feathers while lower officials had only one or two barbules. There were many types of casual hats, with the most common type being "watermelon hat" — a hat of six parts joined at the top. It signifies the union of heaven, earth and all four directions of the world.

long robe for members of the royal family

horse hoof sleeve

four slits on both sides, front and back

watermelon hat

short coat

I am noble

I am ... too !!

Men's dresses in Qing Dynasty included long robe, heavy short coat, shirt, overcoat, pants and others. The long robe and the overcoat are formal dresses. The long robe reaches below the knees and the collar is round. Its front is zipped on the side of the chest with embroidered buttons. There are slits on the robe. Members of the royal family had four slits, while men of official ranking had two. The long robe has an ornamental broad rim shaped like the horse hoof at the end of the sleeve. The rim is usually folded, but it must be flattened while doing courtesy to superiors. The overcoat reaches the waist and is worn over the long robe. It also has a round collar and two slits on the side, with ornamental buttons in the middle or on the side.

The women of Qing Dynasty liked to have the hair piled high into a bun. The rest of the long hair is bound behind the head and trimmed into what looks like the swallow's tail. The bun grew even higher at the end of the Qing Dynasty. An ornamental board was fixed on the head with a huge peony flower in the middle. It was nicknamed "big spreading wings".

Most women wore cloak, heavy coat and skirt for formal occasions. The casual dress would include a long robe embroidered at the collar and sleeve. A vest would add more color and style to the robe. Women of the Han nationality started binding their feet from adolescent years and throughout their lives, they must endure sharp pains walking in narrow, short embroidered shoes that the men very much adored. The Manchurian women were luckier to be free of this bound. But the noble ladies and their maids walked in shoes with a wooden stick shaped like the flower pot at the middle of the sole. It was thought that the women walking gingerly would look more elegant.

Peddlers' call

Carp: Live carp!

Gold fish: Come to buy big and small gold fish!

Tangmianjiao (a dumpling made with half boiled dough and steamed): Hot *tangmian* dumpling!

Yuanxiao (a dumpling made with the powder of glutinous rice for the Lantern Festival): Osmanthus flower *yuanxiao*! Tenacious and smooth! *Yuanxiao* with osmanthus flower and a myriad of flavors!

Taiyanggao (sun cake, a cake printed with the pattern of a cock or with a miniature cock on the top to be offered to the God of Sun on the 1st day of the 2nd lunar month): Sun cake to offer Buddha! Sun cake, sun cake with the cock!

Basins and jars: Small basins! Small jars! Shallow ones for kittens! Jars for water! Chamber pots, big and small!

Xuanfen (bean jelly contained in copper basin known as *tongxuanzi* as a summer dessert): Cool, really cool *xuanfen*!

Chinese prickly ash and Chinese toon: Fresh Chinese prickly ash, tender leaves of Chinese toon!

Common sow thistle: common sow thistle, fresh tender common sow thistle!

Apricot: Apricots, charge you free if it's not sour! Apricots, sweet ones, you can change for free if it's sour!

Chinese herbaceous peony: Chinese herbaceous peony of Imperial Consort Yang (Yang Yuhuan was a favorite imperial Consort of Emperor Xuanzong of Tang Dynasty and one of four best-known beauties in Chinese history).

Yellow croaker: Aye, come and buy yellow croaker!

Zongzi (pyramid-shaped dessert made with glutinous rice wrapped in reed or bamboo leaf for Duanwu Festival): Huge, cool *zongzi* with glutinous rice and small date! Tenacious *zongzi* with glutinous millet and small date!

Calamus and Chinese mugwort (medicinal herbs burnt during the Duanwu Festival to drive away insects and evil spirits): Calamus, good Chinese mugwort!

Mulberry fruit and cherry: Black and white mulberries, big ones to offer to Buddha! Huge cherries! Protective talisman and bottle gourd: Come for talisman to drive away all five poisonous creatures (snake, centipede, scorpion, gecko and toad)!

Steamed lotus root : Lotus root stuffed with glutinous rice!

Sweet-sour plum juice: Really sweet plum juice! Camels carried the spring water from Jade Spring Mountain; bees from the south made the nest. Get a bowl and have a try. I won't charge you if it's not cold or sweet.

Peas: Peas tenacious as cow tendon! Peas that are better than hazelnuts! Dried fragrant peas! Peas better than dried bean curd! Peas! Extra ones! Peas!

Watermelon: Sweet to the core with crispy flesh, what a perfectly round watermelon!

Peach: Big, honey peaches full of juice, honey peaches of Shenzhou (a city in Hebei Province known for good quality peaches)!

Xuehualao (a snowflake-like dessert): Snowflakes falling off icicle drive away summer heat and quench thirst. Snowflakes from icicle, made with good water, sugar and osmanthus flower.

Pear paste candy (the sweet is believed to have a good effect on coughing): Big pear paste candies!

Fresh flowers: Selling magnolia flowers! Jasmine flowers!

Jujube and walnut: Sour jujube, come and buy! It's free if it's not sour!

Crab: Aye-hi-aye, big live crabs!

Hawthorn (the sweet-sour fruits are put on a bamboo stick and dipped in simmering sugar to get a light brown coating): Only two sticks of big hawthorns left!

Peanuts: Crispy peanuts! Come and pick peanuts!

Persimmon: Big persimmons! Like honey! Change it for free if it's astringent.

Cabbage (cabbage used to be the main vegetable for Beijing residents during the long winter, each family would store many before winter came): Store cabbages! Cabbages with green leaves! Store cabbages in cellar!

Charcoal, firewood: Come and get charcoal by each piece! Come and get thoroughly dried firewood!

Lunar calendar: Big calendars! Pictured for each month!

Turnip: Better than pear! Change for free if it's spicy! Crispy turnip, purple and beautiful inside!

Guandong candy (made with malt and millet, it is sold before the Spring Festival as an offering to the God of Stove): Guandong candy!

New Year painting (often in pairs, the painting is put on the front door in the Spring Festival): New Year paintings! Antithetic couplets to put on the door! On courtyard gates, on room doors! If you get a horizontal calligraphy work (for the door lintel to go with the vertical couplets), I'll send you the *fu* (happiness, often put upside down between the couplets to invite good fortune) for free!

Lunar calendar

Transportation in old Beijing

Carts:

Carts driven by horses, donkeys and mules were common in Beijing. Mules became more popular than the other two during the rule of Emperor Qianlong in the 18th century. Mule carts were also available at certain stops along the streets.

Jiaozi (sedan chair):

Originated from chariots, sedan chair was one of the most common means of transportation in Beijing. There were two, four or even eight carriers for one sedan chair according to the social status and affluence of the owner.

Bingchuang (ice bed):

Formed like a sledge with a wooden board over two iron sticks that glide over ice, the ice bed was an old means of transportation and it also gave much fun. The rider would cover the legs with a quilt as the driver propelled the sledge forward. Before the water level became too low in the moat, many people made a living by driving the ice bed.

Rickshaw:

Also called *jinriksha* (*renliche* in Chinese), the cart had hard rubber wheels before pumped tire appeared in the 1900s. Rickshaw Xiangzi, a famous character in Lao She's novel of the same title, was dragging such a new rickshaw. There were tens of thousands of such rickshaws in the 1920s as the chief means of transportation in the city.

Bicycle, tricycle and tramcar

The first bicycles appeared in Beijing during the rule of Emperor Guangxu at the beginning of the 20th century. A folk song describes the novelty: "The rider holds his arms and shoulders high and looks straight ahead. He bends as if making a bow. At a loud sound from behind, the pedestrians all hurry aside to give way to the bicycle."

The tricycle was invented combining the bicycle and the rickshaw. It appeared in 1937 and quickly replaced the rickshaw on the streets.

The tramcar was nicknamed "whistle car" as the driver stepped on a bell with his foot and it whistled. The first tramcars entered into service in 1924 in Beijing.

Train:

Old Beijing residents called train *"qiche"* which means it's a vehicle driven by steam. Another name for train was *"huolunche"* — vehicle on flaming wheels (referring to the burning coals). In 1865 during the rule of Emperor Tongzhi, the British installed a 500-m-long narrow railway outside the Xuanwu Gate. A small engine whistled as it moved. But the Qing court judged this novelty a monster and had the first railway in the country dismantled.

Car:

It wasn't until the 1920s that the first cars began to appear on Beijing's streets. The rare vehicles were reserved for foreign dignitaries. Although public buses appeared in the 1930s, it would take them a long time to become the main medium of public transport.

Ship:

Beijing has always been a transportation hubbub, linking nearby areas with routes both on land and by river. Mules and horses dragged carts along roads to Northeast China from Dongzhimen, to the north and northwest from Deshengmen, and to the south from Lugou Bridge. Outside Chaoyangmen, one could take a boat or walk along the Tonghui River for some 20 km to reach the port at Zhangjiawan in Tongxian (today's Tongzhou District). This is the northern beginning of the Grand Canal that was constructed all the way south to Hangzhou of Jiangsu Province some 1,500 years ago. There were many rivers inside and outside the city, allowing people to sail in boats conveniently. In the Yuan Dynasty, huge cargo ships could sail all the way from eastern China to Jishuitan at the center of Beijing. Sadly, much of the waterway has been destructed in war or neglected. The Beijing municipal government is trying to restore parts of the ancient water system.

Camel:

In the past, camel was an important beast of burden as it is tame and durable. In the 13th century, camels were involved in the construction of Dadu, the name of Beijing given by Kublai Khan as the Grand Capital of the Yuan Dynasty. The worthy animals retired from public sight in the 1950s. For some 700 years, camels had contributed to the founding and prospering of Beijing.

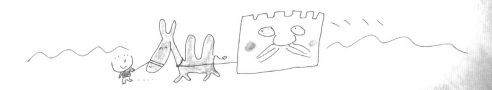

Children's games

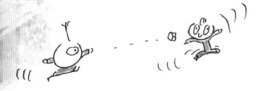

Throwing sandbag

The fist-sized sandbag is made of cloth and contains sand or grain. The player holds the sandbag with both toes and jumps up, throwing it forward as far as possible.

Hitting sandbag

Two lines are drawn on the ground, at 8 or 10 m apart. Two children stand on each line, with a runner between them. The two try to hit the runner. But if the runner catches the sandbag, he or she gains a point.

Shooting glass balls

Some glass balls have three colorful leaves inside while others are just transparent. The player holds the glass ball with the thumb and index finger, then bounces it out toward the five small pits dug on the ground. The one who can get the glass ball into all five pits with the least attempts wins the game.

Whipping a top

The circular cone-shaped spinning top is made of wood and has a small iron ball inlaid at the bottom. It normally measures 6 cm high and 4 cm in diameter. The player whips it on the ground to keep it spinning.

Jumping the rubber band

Two children hold the rubber band or elastic cord about 5 m long. One or more players are required to step on or over the band while singing various tunes that require different dance steps.

Playing the joints

"Guai" refers to the joint of goat's leg. The bone is cleaned and steamed to become a toy. A game needs 4 or 8 joints and a small sandbag. The player throws the joints on the ground, then throws the sandbag up. Before catching the sandbag, the player arranges the joints with the same face to earth. An expert of the game could turn all the joints by throwing the sandbag only once, while the first-timers might fail to turn any joint and miss the sandbag.

Kicking shuttlecock

The shuttlecock is made by binding some feather onto two copper coins. The adroit player can kick it for hundreds of times with his or her feet, knees, shoulders, forehead and not resolve to the arms.

Flapping pictures

Some foreign and local companies used to issue mini-pictures promoting their products. The children found the cards enjoyable toys. Some pictures portray characters in *Romance of the Three Kingdoms* and other classic novels. The player hits the ground where the pictures are scattered and the air would flip the pictures around. Then the player would sway the hand to keep the pictures turning.

Hotlines, accommodation, transportation, recreation

Hotlines

Beijing mayor's hotline: 65128080
Beijing tourism hotline: 65130828
Police: 110
Information: 114
Fire alarm: 119
Medical emergency: 120
Traffic: 122
Red Cross: 999
Taxi service: 68373399
Aviation information/booking service: 2580/2581
Beijing Railway Station Information Service: 51019999
Beijing Western Railway Station Information Service: 51826273
Li Suli Transportation Hotline: 96166
Beijing Evening News Hotline: 65298020

Concert halls

Beijing Concert Hall:No 1, Beixinhua Street, 66057006
Zhongshan Concert Hall: Zhongshan Park to the west of the Forbidden City, 66056059

Fishing sites

Daoxiang Fishing Garden

Covering 0.5 sq km, the garden raises rare fish species and provides anglers some good spots to spend their time.
Add: to the west of Daoxiang Lake, Xixiaoying Town, Sujiasuo, Haidian District

Beijing Fishing Courtyard

Visitors can lodge at classical *siheyuan* courtyards, dine at the central hall and participate in business meetings at any of the stylish villas.

Jinxiu Fishing Village

Sheltered by a hill and nestled near water, the village has many fruit trees. The water surface of 0.1 sq km has springs and ample fish for anglers to spend both day and night.
Add: Suyukou Reservoir, Yukou Village, Qiaozi Town, Huairou District
Tel: 69675450, 69675452

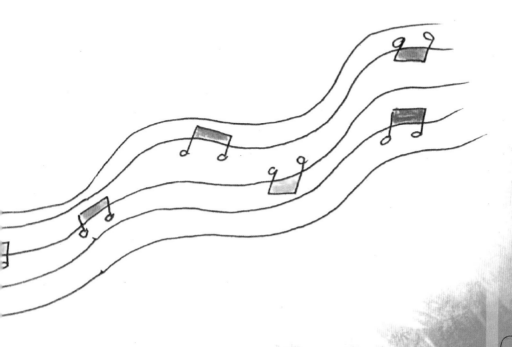

Franchised hotels

Jinjiang Inns Ltd Co: 021-51691218
Super 8 Hotel: 400-810-7822
Home Inn: 4008203333
7 Days Inn: 400 880 7777
Xinyandu Hotel: 66166661

Transportation

Aviation: Beijing is the hubbub of domestic and international aviation. The Capital Airport is 30 km away from downtown Beijing and linked with many shuttle buses, an expressway and a light rail that entered operation in 2008.

Railway: As the national railway center, Beijing has five railway stations for passengers. Besides the old Beijing Railway Station and Beijing West Railway Station, which is the biggest railway station in Asia, there are also the northern, southern and Fengtai railway stations.

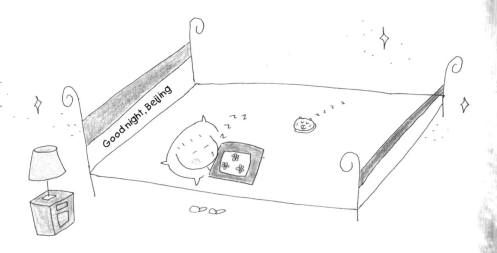

Good night, Beijing

Picking fruits

Peach at Pinggu District
Tel: 69980550, 89991180

Walnut at Huairou District
Tel: 61621954, 61621148

Cherry at Shuanghe Orchard, Hebei Village, Nancai Town, Shunyi District
Tel: 89477712

Persimmons at Zhangfang, Fangshan District
Tel: 6133628, 61338228

Wild mushroom, Zhenzhuhu Township, Yanqing District
Tel: 60186388

Watermelon at Panggezhuang
Tel: 89288545

Persimmons at Shisanling
Add: Shisanling (Ming Dynasty Tombs) area of Changping District

Opera houses

Beijing People's Art Theater

Beijing People's Art Theater was founded in 1952 with Cao Yu (1910-1996) as the first president. The first show staged here was *Longxugou (Dragon Beard Ditch)* by renowned writer Lao She. In following years, grand dramas like *Leiyu (Thunderstorm)*, *Richu (Sun Rise)*, *Beijing Ren (Beijinger)*, *Hufu (Tiger Tally)*, *Chaguan (Teahouse)*, *Cai Wenji*, *Luotuo Xiangzi (Rickshaw Xiangzi)* and *Aesop* were staged at the theater. Jiao Juyin, Ouyang Shanzun, Yu Shizhi and many other dramatists, actors and actresses, as well as stage artists gained national stardom at the venue. The dramas at this theater have been seen as classics of modern Chinese drama.

Chang'an Grand Theater

First founded in 1937, the renovated theater is located on the first floor of the Guanghua Chang'an Building to the north of the Chang'an Avenue. It combines classic and modern architectural elements in the sandalwood tables and soft seats. The house can hold 800 audience and most shows are from classic repertoire of folk operas.

Lao She Teahouse

At Qianmen West Street, the renowned teahouse is named after Lao She, a great writer who depicted old Beijing's life. The bronze bust of the writer beneath the teahouse's name plate gazes into the distance, giving the venue an air of literature and art. Besides savoring tea and folk snacks, visitors can enjoy dazzling performances with distinct Chinese flavor every night.

Jixiang Theater

Located to the north of Dong'an Market in Wangfujing, Jixiang Theater was built in 1906 by Liu Xiezhi and witnessed the performance of many heavy-weight Peking Opera masters. The new theater provides both Peking Opera live shows and movies. Its advantageous location has guaranteed a prosperous business.

Liyuan Theater

The Liyuan Theater is the first performance hall opened by Beijing Qianmen Hotel and Peking Opera House of Beijing. The world-renowned Peking Opera Troupe of Beijing gives a nightly performance here with many famous actors and actresses. The audience can savor local Beijing snacks and sip tea to enjoy the classic repertoire. The exhibition hall introduces the history of Peking Opera and celebrated masters. Aficionados can also buy costumes, facial masks and musical instruments.

Huguang Guild Theater

Located at No 3 of Hufang Street in Xuanwu District, the guild was built in 1807 to receive officials in Hunan and Hubei provinces when they visited the capital. Today it has become the Beijing Opera Museum. Yu Shuyan, Mei Lanfang and numerous other masters of Peking Opera and other arts left traces here. Every Saturday, opera fans would join masters to stage a show that features some of Peking Opera's best-known arias.

Tianqiaole Tea Garden

The Tianle Opera House was first founded in 1933. Tea garden was the venue for old Beijing residents to admire Peking Opera. The Tianqiaole Tea Garden is modeled upon old-style tea garden and opera house to stage folk operas, folk art performances and martial arts. Tianqiao used to be a boisterous place where people could find all sorts of recreation. The tea garden seeks to bring back the glorious past on stage.

Zhengyici Opera House

The 300-year-old wooden architecture is located near the Tian'anmen Square at No 220, Xiheyan of Qianmen. Covering 1,000 sq m of floor space, it allows audience to sit on three sides of the stage. The front side has tables for some 200 audience to sip tea and enjoy the show. There are two layers of boxes fanning the stage.

Bravo!!

Amusement parks

Old Beijing Miniature Garden

The garden at Hongnigou of Nankou Town in Changping District captures typical scenes of Beijing in the Ming and Qing dynasties. The Forbidden City, *hutong* lanes and *siheyuan* courtyards are rebuilt on a mini-scale but with meticulous details.

Shijingshan Amusement Park

The amusement park at Bajiao Village of Shijingshan District features Western castles with statues from fairy tales such as Cinderella, Mickey Mouse and Donald Duck. There are more than 20 facilities in the park such as merry-go-round, rollercoaster, race car and fairytale train.

Beijing Amusement Park

Built at the middle lake of Longtanhu Park in southern Chongwen District, the park was the first of its kind in Beijing. The island has a sightseeing lift that can raise the visitor to 60 m into the air. There are also a giant wheel and gliding rails.

Beijing Film Tourism City

Built inside Beijing Film Studio at Beitaipingzhuang, the recreational site has a street that displays Ming and Qing dynasties' social customs, the residences of Rong and Ning families constructed for the shooting of *A Dream of the Red Chamber*, a gallery of movie arts and a studio showing thriller productions. The site brings visitors a fresh understanding of the film industry.

Beijing Fuguo Undersea World

At the southern gate of Worker's Stadium, the aquarium has the longest underwater channel in Asia. Visitors can watch some 6,000 awesome marine creatures swimming around. The staff will demonstrate feeding sharks and the dance of mermaids.

China North International Shooting Range

To the north of Mafang Village, Nankou Town of Changping District, one can find China's first recreational shooting range. Here one can try a hand at pistol, rifle, machine-gun and even rocket-launcher. The exhibition hall displays advanced light weapons in the world.

Wax Sculpture Museum of Ming Dynasty

Built close to the Ming Dynasty imperial tombs, the museum has 374 wax sculptures grouped in 26 scenes that relate the history of Ming Dynasty (1368-1644). From Zhu Yuanzhang who founded Ming Dynasty to the last Ming emperor Chongzhen who hanged himself, the sculptures capture all the important events in the dynasty.

Miyun International Amusement Park

This is the biggest modern amusement park in Beijing installed with the ferric wheel, single-railed train and a horse race ground.

Primitive Tribes Park

Hidden in deep mountains about 12 km away from Huairou District, the park provides performances of the ancient shaman religion. At the earthen huts of primitive tribes, visitors can find frescoes, relief sculptures, wood carvings and stone piles.

Seasons of blossoms

Peach blossom in Pinggu

April 15 is the Peach Blossom Festival in Pinggu District.

Pear blossom in Daxing

Panggezhuang of Daxing has some 20 sq km of pear farms. There are many kinds of pear flowers that burst into blossom in spring.

Flowers at Jiufeng

Jiufeng Peak becomes a world of flowers in spring, with Chinese plum, peach, apricot and magnolia blooming in succeeding weeks. One can drive along the Badaling Highway, turn out at Bei'anhe Exit towards Beiqing Road before finding the peak.

Roses at Miaofeng Mountain

The rose valley at Miaofeng Mountain is said to accommodate the best kinds of rose in North China. One can drive along Fushi Street, turn right at Shuangyulu Roundabout, then follow the No 109 State Road before finding the mountain.

Peony in Huairou

The Peony Garden at Qiaozi Town of Huairou District covers 2.3 sq km. It is home to more than 1 million peonies of 600 types.

Apricot flower at Fenghuangling

In April, the apricot trees become flowery at Fenghuangling (Phoenix Range). One can drive along the Badaling Highway, turn off at Bei'anhe Exit towards Beiqing Road before finding the site.

Magnolia at Tangzhe Temple

The magnolia trees at the ancient temple become giant towers of white and purple flowers in early spring.

Magnolia at Dajue Temple

The magnolias at Dajue Temple of the West Hill are known for their perfect shape and pure color.

Sightseeing and picking fruits

Jinxiudadi Agriculture Garden

Add: No 166, Liaogongzhuan, Haidian District
Tel: 88702172

Badaling Modern Agriculture Garden

Add: Badaling Town, Yanqing County
Tel: 69141463
Driving route: along the Badaling Highway

Hancunhe Village

Add: Hancunhe Village, Fangshan District, about 40 km from downtown Beijing
Tel: 80380015
Driving route: along Jingshi Highway, turn out at Liulihe Exit

Xiedao Resort

Add: No 1, Xiedao Street, Jinzhan Township, Chaoyang District
Tel: 84311865

Xiaotangshan Modern Agricultural Technique Garden

Add: Xiaotangshan Town, Changping District
Driving route: at Daliushu Roundabout of Xiaotangshan Town, turn south, drive 2,000 m to Mafang Bridge, follow the northern bank of Wenyu River and drive for 20 km toward east

Skiing grounds

Badaling Ski Field

Add: About 2,000 m to the west of Badaling Section of the Great Wall
Tel: 89761886
Driving route: drive along Badaling Highway, turn out at Badaling Exit, turn left at the parking lot's exit and drive for 3,000 m towards west

Huaibei International Skiing Ground

Add: No 48, Fangkou Village, Huaibei Town, Huairou District
Tel: 69661177, 69666712
Driving route: drive along Jingshun Road to Huairou City, passing by Fule Roundabout to reach Fangkou Village of Huaibei Town

Shijinglong Ski Field

Add: 1 km away from the west of Huangbaisi Village, Yanqing County
Tel: 69191615
Driving route: take Badaling Highway to Yanqing County, follow the Longqingxia Section of the No 110 State Road to Huangbaisi Village, drive 1 km towards west

Hot springs

Xiaotangshan Longmai Hot Spring (Longmai Hot Spring Resort)

Add: Xiaotangshan Town, Changping District
Tel: 61780121, 61782465
Driving route: take Jingchang Highway, turn out at Xiaotangshan Exit, drive 12 km to the east to the central street of Xiaotangshan Town, turn left at the building of Industrial and Commercial Bank

Jiuhua Hot Spring (Jiuhua Resort)

Add: Xiaotangshan Town, Changping District
Tel: 61784890, 61784887
Driving route: from Lishuiqiao, drive north till Daliushu Roundabout, turn east for 500 m; or drive along Jingcheng or Badaling highways to reach the roundabout.

Tianye Hot Spring Resort

Add: west of Post Office, Xiaotangshan Town, Changping District
Tel: 61781166
Driving route: from Anzhenqiao, drive north along Ansi Road to reach Daliushu Roundabout, turn left towards Xiaotangshan Town

Yutangquan Resort

Add: Mafang, Xiaotangshan Town, Changping District
Tel: 86219099
Driving route: from Anzhenqiao, drive north along Ansi Road, turn right at Mafangdongqiao

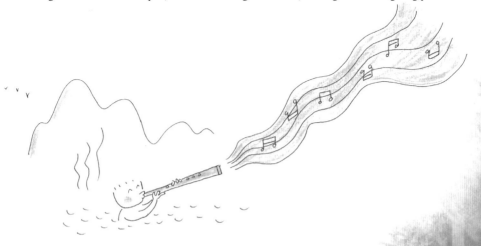

图书在版编目（CIP）数据

漫画旅行北京：英文/王麒诚著 刘浚译.
—北京：五洲传播出版社，2009.5
ISBN 978-7-5085-1530-4

Ⅰ.漫... Ⅱ.①王...②刘... Ⅲ.北京市-概况-英文 Ⅳ.K291.64

中国版本图书馆CIP数据核字（2009）第052506号

著　　者：王麒诚
主　　编：荆孝敏
英文翻译：刘　浚

责任编辑：张美景
设计总监：闫志杰
封面设计：谢敬一
设计制作：申真真

出　　版：五洲传播出版社
发　　行：五洲传播出版社
地　　址：北京市海淀区北小马厂6号华天大厦
邮　　编：100038
网　　址：www.cicc.org.cn
电　　话：010-58891281
印　　刷：北京正合鼎业印刷技术有限公司
开　　本：787×1092mm　1/32
印　　张：5.5
版　　次：2009年5月第1版　2009年5月第1次印刷
书　　号：ISBN 978-7-5085-1530-4
定　　价：89.00元